W9-DJA-874

CHAMELEON

The True Story of an Impostor's
Remarkable Odyssey

By Robert Brandt

MOORESVILLE PUBLIC LIBRARY
220 W. HARRISON ST.
MOORESVILLE, IN 46158
317-831-7323

Copyright © 2013 Robert Brandt
All rights reserved.

ISBN: 1493509470
ISBN 13: 9781493509478
Library of Congress Control Number: 2013920116
CreateSpace Independent Publishing Platform
North Charleston, South Carolina

TABLE OF CONTENTS

Chapter 1	The Crime	1
Chapter 2	Caracas	17
Chapter 3	Return to the Scene of the Crime	29
Chapter 4	Our Man in La Guaira	43
Chapter 5	Minister McGoodwin	53
Chapter 6	Great Escape I	65
Chapter 7	The Consul's Treachery	77
Chapter 8	Great Escape II	89
Chapter 9	One More Chance	101
Chapter 10	The Gathering Storm	113
Chapter 11	War Is Hell	121
Chapter 12	When the Spies Came	133
Chapter 13	Mission Aborted	141
Chapter 14	The Editor	153
Chapter 15	Uh-Oh	165
Chapter 16	The Oil Business	175
Chapter 17	Toppling the Minister	185
Chapter 18	All the President's Men	197
Chapter 19	THISCLOSE	209
Chapter 20	A Death in the Family	219

Chapter 21   Something Old, Something New   227
Chapter 22   The Final Chapter   251
              Epilogue   255
              Notes   277
              Acknowledgments   289
              About the Author   293

On the Cover: Henry Sanger Snow, alias Cyrus N. Clark, is the Chameleon, shown on the cover posing for a *Gaceta Oficial* photograph in Caracas after receiving the Order of the Liberator from the Venezuelan government on Sept. 21, 1920. The award was presented by General Ignacio Andrade Troconis, at the time Chameleon's closest ally inside the government.

THE CRIME

It was 1908. It was a leap year, and the first New Year to be reigned in with the dropping of the ball at Times Square. It was a presidential election year. William Howard Taft was running against William Jennings Bryan. The nation was still struggling to pull out of the financial abyss that was known as the Panic of 1907. New York's leading bankers had spent much of the previous fall holed up in J. P. Morgan's personal library, summoned there time and again by the great financier to stem collapse of the nation's financial system. In Brooklyn Heights, one of the city's elite was suffering his own financial crash and it, too, was Page One news.

Henry Sanger Snow's difficulties first came to the public attention on February 10 with the delivery of the day's edition of the *Brooklyn Eagle*, the borough's fabled afternoon newspaper.

The distinguished and respected treasurer of the New York and New Jersey Telephone Company was out of a job. While this statement was true, the *Eagle* had missed the point completely. Several newspaper stories in the ensuing days would also miss the point. Without citing a named source, the *Eagle* reported that Snow had lost out after a recent merger of the company. It reported that a "Manhattan element" had succeeded in gaining control of the company.

Snow immediately reached out to reporters, misleading them into believing that his resignation was routine and expected. He denied that any friction over the merger existed within the company.

Snow said, "For some time changes have been contemplated in connection with the two companies, and my resignation marks the beginning of the execution of the new plans."

He hoped to buy some time before his wife and four children began to ask questions. He owed creditors a fortune and he knew they were already asking questions.

Snow's boyhood in Brooklyn was one of privilege. He first came to public notice when he was named valedictorian of Brooklyn Polytechnic Institute in 1878.

After graduating, he entered law school at Columbia University. He later received a master's degree in law from New York University. His legal career spanned two decades, and he spent much of it on Wall Street. As a business and civics leader, he was frequently mentioned in the press, most often glowing references to his leadership roles on the boards of city libraries or his brilliant stewardship as president and chairman of his beloved Polytechnic Institute.

He was fifty-one years old, although he appeared much younger, with a youthful face and what one reporter described as "a slight, active springy frame." He'd already retired from his legal career.

Snow's social and professional stature made him one of the most recognized men in the Heights. The events that he hosted were described in the press as lavish. Luminaries representing Wall Street, the banking community, and academia were guests at his dinner on one particular evening. Snow would later tell his children that the diners represented a combined wealth, including Snow, of fifty million dollars.

The coming-out party of Marion, Snow's eldest daughter, was one of the most costly parties that anybody had ever thrown in Brooklyn. The family's brownstone at 270 Henry Street was on the "block beautiful." It was located between Joralemon Street and State Street, and Snow's neighbors were counted among the city's most distinguished residents.

The newspapers depicted Snow as a man of great wealth who ran his house on a "grand scale" and who was frequently seen riding around town in his topless automobile. Snow's house had three, and at times four, full-time staff members, including a chauffeur.

He had numerous club memberships. Snow served on the executive committee of the New York Civil Service Reform Association and he belonged to the Hamilton, Marine, and Field Club and the Dyker Meadow Golf Club. He was a trustee of the Nassau Trust Company, and he had once been a director of the Ottawa & New York Railway. He was an energetic man who stayed busy.

On the second day of its coverage, the *Eagle* began to chip away at the real story behind Henry Snow. A headline on page one read, "Henry Sanger Snow Crippled Financially." The newspaper reported that his resignation from the telephone company had caused much surprise in financial circles. However, Snow had indicated that his troubles were only temporary. He continued to dupe reporters, knowing that his troubles were not at all temporary.

After his investments had collapsed, Snow borrowed deeply from a number of local financial institutions. With his fortunes continuing to slide, he'd been forced to negotiate further loans to carry him through the crisis. The telephone company directors became aware of the loans, and they were conducting a company audit. Unsure of the outcome, a spokesman maintained that it was routine. He claimed that the audit was not related to Snow's resignation. It is likely the spokesman knew otherwise.

Following Snow's example, Snow's friends attempted to explain away his heavy borrowing. One of his friends, quoted anonymously, said, "It was not unusual for a man to be financially embarrassed at the present time."

The friends all voiced optimism that Snow would be able to extricate himself from his "embarrassment."

Publicly, Snow remained even more optimistic. He used words to assuage reporters, telephone company officials, law enforcement officials, his neighbors, his friends, and his family.

"I expect to have my affairs straightened out in the near future," he told reporters. "When my affairs are adjusted, I may have more to say."

If he was losing confidence, he didn't show it. He remained calm and gave no sign that his circumstances were far worse than his bland responses indicated.

Snow's financial downfall had been years in the making. It had resulted partly from the family's expensive lifestyle. More significantly, Snow had invested in the railroad company of which he was a director. Snow and his close friend, an attorney named Burnham Moffat, represented the New York & Ottawa Railroad in 1897. They applied to extend the company's service from Moira, New York, to the St. Lawrence River. Snow negotiated with Canadian officials to build a bridge across the river. This would shorten the route from New York City to Ottawa by fifty miles. The bridge project required congressional legislation, and Snow traveled to Washington to push the bill through.

During the construction of the bridge, calamity struck. Two great spans collapsed, killing fifteen laborers. The spans sank to the river bottom and they had to be raised. New construction was able to finish the project, but the accident forced the railroad company into receivership in 1900. When it foreclosed in 1902, it owed more than two million dollars. It was sold in 1904.

Snow's friends, who were widely quoted but never named in the press, regarded him as a cautious investor. They were unaware that his speculation in the stock market had taken a more aggressive turn after his railroad company had failed. Nobody knew about the complex borrowing scheme that he used to take stock positions. He was cashing in bonds coming from the telephone company's sinking fund, rather than depositing it to pay off company debts.

Snow's friends informed reporters that he had recently acquired a summer home on Lake George in upstate New York. One of his friends also mentioned "a country place he is known to have purchased in Connecticut last spring." They implied that Snow couldn't possibly be in real financial danger.

Wednesday was Lincoln's Birthday. Despite the holiday, the telephone company's top executives gathered at its offices on Dey Street in Manhattan. The group included the company's president, U. N. Bethell. He had come to the city from his home in Morristown, New Jersey. Several of the other top executives arrived at the offices soon thereafter. After a long consultation behind closed doors, Bethell sent his secretary to inform the assembled press that the company would have no new statement about Snow's resignation.

Snow remained available to the press, and he used the reporters to his advantage.

One reporter said to Snow, "In your statement, you admitted that you were temporarily embarrassed as to your private affairs. By that, you mean that only your private affairs are involved, do you not?"

"I hope so," Snow responded. "I hope that I shall get fixed out all right in the near future."

Snow felt comfortable responding to questions, but he was evasive, deceptive, and dishonest. He spent more than a week downplaying and misrepresenting his problems. He would make a circus of the newspapers, even though the *Eagle* needed no help with this.

Over thirteen days, the *Eagle* ran fourteen stories on Snow. Many of them were on the front page. Snow lived right in the heart of the newspaper's primary area of circulation, and many of its readers recognized his name. The *New York Times* and the *New York Tribune* were less aggressive. Once the salacious details emerged, though, they, too, began to carry daily stories. Newspapers outside of the city ran stories on Snow too.

The police tried to keep Snow under surveillance, but it became clear over several days that their success was minimal. Dashing around the city, Snow called on friends. He hoped to borrow funds from them, and he enlisted them to serve as intermediaries with the police. He frequently and steadily assured them that he was nearby and prevailed on them to deliver that message to police.

On Thursday, February 13, Snow's photograph appeared at the top of the *Eagle's* front page. He was wearing his trademark shirt with a high standing collar. His thick hair was parted down the middle. His moustache turned slightly upward at each end. To his wife's distress, Snow's financial wrongdoings, which were substantial, were being detailed for all to read. The accompanying news story revealed that the telephone company's board of directors was informed that one hundred eighty thousand dollars was missing from the company's accounts. Mrs. Snow took immediately to her bed.

Snow's photograph in the newspaper had increased his risk of being recognized, but Snow remained anonymously at large. When reporters ran down his attorney at his New York offices, their avalanche of questions unnerved him. The Snow's attorney was Snow's good friend, Moffat. Moffat had been his partner in the failed railroad company. He wasn't used to reporters' prying. He became agitated immediately, and he remarked stiffly that it was the first time he had ever been involved in a criminal case. He said, "I hope it will be the last time." The significance of the attorney calling it a criminal case was noted but otherwise not picked up on by the press.

Moffat concluded the interview with a brusque, "Nothing to say. Nothing to say. Nothing means nothing—big N." Withdrawing to his inner office, he closed the door and remained inside until the reporters departed.

On the morning of Friday, February 14, Snow was indicted for grand larceny in the first degree. Twenty-nine thousand dollars in one lot of company bonds were missing along with another lot of bonds for ten thousand dollars. One hundred forty-six thousand dollars in company stock were also missing. Newspaper stories confirmed that the bonds should have been applied against the company's sinking fund.

As the indictment explained, Snow "didn't send them to the trust company as he should have, but deposited them with several financial institutions as collateral for personal loans or as margin for stock market transactions."

The New York Tribune joined the fray on Friday. They ran a front-page story that indicated that Snow's financial irregularities amounted to about one hundred fifty thousand dollars. A company director said that Snow had offered to make up any shortage of funds.

According to the indictment, Snow had begun embezzling four or five years before, the time during which the railroad company was going through foreclosure and forced sale.

With the indictment and an arrest warrant in hand, two detectives knocked on the door of the Snow home on Henry Street around noon on Friday. Marion, Snow's eldest, most mature, and most polished child, answered the door and told the officers that Snow wasn't there. She then escorted them through the house so that they could see for themselves. They even went to the room where Snow's wife, Anna Laconte Brooks Snow lay ill on her bed. Anna was the daughter of noted inventor and telegrapher David Brooks. She was the former national president of the General Society of the Daughters of the Revolution, and she was the president of its Long Island branch. Anna was under the care of a doctor.

The house had been under watch by two detectives throughout Thursday night. The detectives said Marion had been overheard telling a household servant that "Father says he is not at home to anybody tonight." The detectives said that they were certain that Snow had not emerged from the house after their arrival the evening before. Snow had not only used his friends to fool police into thinking that he would imminently surrender. He had also used his daughter to deceive police into thinking that he was at home that night.

Over the next several days, Snow's friends continued to calm the police with claims that his surrender would come at any moment. Day after day, the headlines reflected the same theme: "Expect Snow to Appear When He Arranges Bail." Another headline said, "Snow to Surrender Today." Another headline said, "Snow Is Negotiating For a Return Home."

As police combed the city to find Snow, Brooklyn District Attorney John F. Clarke and Captain August Kuhne of the Brooklyn Detective Bureau indicated that they were fully confident that Snow was nearby. They continued to accept the word of his friends, quoting one of them saying "that Snow has never at any time meditated flight, but was simply evading the police until arrangements could be completed among his friends to get the necessary bail for his release." The friends called on the district attorney's office, asking that Snow's bail not be excessive. The newspapers reported that Snow had wished to avoid being "measured" and "having his photograph made for the Rogues Gallery."

Over the weekend following the indictment, Kuhne reconsidered. By Monday his confidence clearly was wavering. Appearing before reporters, he was rattled. Out of the blue, he proclaimed that he'd changed his mind that morning. He said that he now believed that Snow had fled the city. Kuhne told the reporters that Snow had likely fled the moment when the newspapers had revealed information about his "irregularities with the telephone company."

Kuhne now revealed that police were considering the possibility that Snow had fled the country. The police had learned that only two ships had sailed on the previous Thursday. This was the last time that Snow had been seen by eyewitnesses. The earliest ship had departed at 10:00 a.m. for France. It was too early for Snow to have caught it, the police concluded. They believed that he had been at home at that hour. Another ship had left in the afternoon for Havana. Police believed that he would have had time to catch that ship.

Captain Kuhne's public recitals of the circumstances of Snow's disappearance took on a life of their own. His statements about Snow's disappearance turned out to be no better than his amateurish investigation and his surveillance of Snow. He first told reporters that Snow had gathered a few possessions from his stately mansion on the night of February 13. Snow had left and stole away into the cold, damp night. Two policemen standing under streetlights along Henry Street in front of the house were unaware as Snow crept out the back door to a stoop, walked silently across it, and stepped over a rail to his neighbor's porch. From there, he made his way to freedom.

Captain Kuhne simultaneously announced that he had assigned ten men to the case. He had directed them not to return to headquarters until they had caught Snow. Kuhne said that he was convinced that Snow had already fled the city. He said that Snow had possibly fled the country. He announced that the telephone company had hired fifty Pinkerton detectives who were "scouring the city for clues to his whereabouts." An equal number of them were "guarding the ferry slips and railroad stations in the hope of preventing his escape."

The police scoffed at the suggestion that Snow had committed suicide. They declared that Snow was "not a man of the temperament to kill himself."

Kuhne soon confused reporters further. According to his new account, someone had observed Snow leaving his house in a horse-drawn cab. He had carried a steamer trunk and other luggage. The headline read, "Snow Took a Trunk When He Fled Town." The author of the article speculated that Snow "went away prepared to stay a long time." In the newest account, Snow departed his home for the last time on Thursday, February 13. He had left the night before his indictment when the two policemen were supposed to be guarding the front of the house.

Kuhne based his claims on "incontrovertible authority" from an eyewitness who had seen the cab pull up to the house. The driver remained atop the cab for five minutes. Then someone opened the front door of Snow's home. Snow emerged. He was bundled in a heavy fur overcoat. Kuhne quoted an eyewitness's description of the scene. Snow moved rapidly down the stoop and walked to the cab. Several family members huddled in the front door as "a large steamer trunk, which I judge was filled to its capacity, as the men who were lifting it seemed to be exerting themselves, was placed on the cab." Once they had secured it, Snow stepped into the cab and closed the door.

The eyewitness was quoted saying that the driver, "whipped up his horse and drove away toward Atlantic Avenue. The women at the front door, one of whom I think was Marion, all waved their handkerchiefs as the cab disappeared down the street."

The eyewitness said Snow was carrying jewelry that belonged to his wife and daughters when he fled the house.

As detailed as this description was, Kuhne dismissed it the next day. A more thorough investigation, he stated, found no basis for the report. He attempted to put an end to these specious reports. He gave a new account.

This time, he claimed that Snow had disappeared from his house on the morning of Thursday, February 13. He had left at 10:30 a.m. He had walked to the subway station at Borough Hall, where he had caught a subway into Manhattan.

"I know that this is so," Kuhne said, "because Mr. Adams of Brooklyn Life saw Mr. Snow standing on the station platform about 10:40 o'clock and subsequently saw him enter a Manhattan-bound train. I have traced Snow's movements pretty much throughout the day and evening. He went to a prominent Wall Street man in the afternoon and tried to borrow twenty-five thousand dollars in cash, but he was not successful. In the evening, he visited another friend at his home across the river. After Snow left that friend's house, he apparently disappeared."

It wasn't the last time that Kuhne would change his story. His later reports added nothing to the facts.

Anna Snow's first and only statement supported the claim that Snow had left the house for the last time on Thursday morning, February 13.

"I do not know where Mr. Snow is. I haven't the faintest idea of his present whereabouts. I have neither seen nor heard from him since he left home on Thursday morning, presumably to visit his lawyer in Manhattan. If I did know where Mr. Snow was, I would impart my knowledge to those who are making inquiries."

Kuhne continued to prevent the police from distributing circulars nationwide. These circulars contained Snow's photograph and a description of his appearance. It wasn't necessary, he explained to reporters.

Kuhne's explanation thoroughly contradicted past accounts that Snow had fled and was possibly outside the United States.

"It is my opinion, based on careful investigation of the case, that Snow is either in or near the city, and I believe that he will surrender himself or be arrested in the near future. The idea that Snow has fled to distant parts is in my mind absurd. Everything points to the opposite," Captain Kuhne stoically remarked.

A spokesman for the district attorney said, "I am inclined to believe that Snow is not very far away." The spokesman acknowledged that he had no real evidence to support this claim, but he cited "his general knowledge of Snow's character." He didn't stop there. "Snow is the kind of a man whose nature would drive him irresistibly back to this borough. He is a finely educated, sensitive man. His family, his home, his friends, all his ties are here and I do not believe he could remain away long, even if he wanted to."

Telephone company officials also believed that Snow hadn't left the city. They believed that he was staying at a friend's home, and they believed that police were watching this home.

By Saturday, February 22, Kuhne's misplaced trust had collapsed. Snow had not shown up, and reports of his whereabouts were contradictory. The detective concluded that Snow had probably fled New York. He ordered the police department to create circulars and send them out to cities in the United States, Canada, and Europe. The circulars carried Snow's photograph, along with the following description:

"Henry Sanger Snow, former treasurer of the New York & New Jersey Telephone Company, is wanted in Brooklyn, Kings County, State of New York, for grand larceny; is about fifty years of age; about five feet eight inches in height; slim build, weighs about one-hundred-and-fifty pounds; thin face, and complexion may be described as sallow; black hair; eyes light brown; wore a moustache when last seen in Brooklyn, but may remove it to disguise himself; carries himself erect; springy walk and active in his movements; may be described as somewhat nervous; has long neck and usually wears high standing collars; dresses neatly. He is well educated, very fluent speaker, accomplished, and refined. He is a lawyer, and was president of the Polytechnic Institute of Brooklyn at one time."

Incredibly, Snow had all the time that he needed.

It was revealed a month after his disappearance that Snow had called at his mother's house before his resignation from the telephone company. D. Maria Snow was an invalid and would survive only one more month. With two other witnesses at her bedside, Snow had instructed her to sign a revised will. She no longer left her estate to him. She left it to Anna, his wife. A servant, a caretaker for Anna, and Henry Snow witnessed the signing of the will. Snow had apparently written it, and his mother had signed it on February 7, 1908. This happened three days before the telephone company announced that it was terminating Snow.

Friends of Snow explained that they "believed that Snow, realizing that exposure was inevitable, and wishing to make some provision for his wife, whose property he had looted, persuaded his mother to destroy a former will, made in his favor, and execute a new one in favor of his wife."

The press speculated that Snow didn't tell his mother the reason for the new will. He apparently thought that it would have been unnecessary, as she was feeble at the time of his visit. She was "so feeble, in fact, that the news of her son's transgressions was never told to her out of fear that the shock would cause instant death."

The newspapers quoted lawyers as saying that Snow had kept his mother's estate out of the reach of his creditors. "Had the property been willed to him, the telephone company and many other financial institutions to which he is indebted could have attached the estate on the mother's death. Now it is safely out of grasp of all outsiders." Still, the newspapers reported that Mrs. Anna Snow "was left practically destitute."

Intimate friends of the family told reporters that the estate of Snow's mother was "practically wiped out" as well.

"It was doubtful it would amount to more than ten thousand dollars or fifteen thousand dollars," one was quoted.

Snow's mother had retained the family home at 114 Lafayette Avenue in Brooklyn. According to press accounts, it was heavily mortgaged. Her husband, Michael Snow, was a partner in a New York business that exported dry goods. He had apparently left "considerable property." Alluding to the time before the stock market crash, the press noted that her estate had been "greatly increased through the efforts of the widow's son." Now it was mostly gone. Fellow members of the Hamilton Club, where Snow was the chairman of the House Committee, were so enraged about the charges that they called on police to protest that "A grave error has been made, a very grave error. Mr. Snow could not possibly have committed the acts he is alleged to have done." One friend explained that Snow had been the "ethical referee" of the dining club and that "delicate questions of ethics which arose during conversations at the club were always submitted to him."

In their final accounting of Snow's embezzlement, the telephone company reported that Snow had stolen exactly $139,370.72. It said that he had misappropriated twenty-nine thousand dollars in company bonds, putting the sum of the "irregularities" at $168,370.72.

The telephone company had recovered twenty thousand dollars from the agent who had bonded Snow, and it had recovered thirty thousand dollars in equity in collateral on Snow's personal loans. Its losses were $118,370.72.

Snow had never considered the possibility of turning himself in, facing a trial, or risking imprisonment. He knew that he would miss living with his family, but he could not envision Anna and the children visiting him in prison. He could never have allowed it. His finances were in steep decline, and he would be unable to produce any income while in prison or after. He would be of no economic value to his family now or later. Who would hire him after a prison term? He didn't like his chances to avoid being convicted and going to prison and he couldn't face the humiliation. It

15 MOORESVILLE PUBLIC LIBRARY
220 WEST HARRISON STREET
MOORESVILLE, INDIANA 46158

was better for him to disappear. Henry Sanger Snow believed that he deserved better.

He left behind Anna, his three daughters, and his son. Marion, his favorite child, was twenty-one years old. Edward Leslie, who had been named after Snow's brother, was fifteen years old. Daughter Anna, called Anne by family members, was twelve years old, and Constance was five.

Snow had plundered a handsome sum over several years. It was the equivalent of three and a half million dollars in today's dollars. What was left of this amount was unknown. It was possible that nothing was left. Snow had gotten rid of all encumbrances, including the police. He couldn't have known where his path would take him or what he would have to do to survive. The man who had worked himself up with his "engaging personality" would have much to overcome. Henry Sanger Snow, valedictorian, lawyer, educator, investor, company treasurer, husband, and father of four, was now also a fugitive.

MOORESVILLE PUBLIC LIBRARY
220 WEST HARRISON STREET
MOORESVILLE, INDIANA 46158

2

CARACAS

> With aspect secret, visage dark,
> Behold the deep, conspiring CLARK;
> He sleeps and rises, comes and goes,
> But what he's after, no one knows.
> Concessions, revolutions, graft,
> Or inside news from Mr. Taft?
> Grave diplomats hang on his words,
> He gathers bolas from the birds;
> Hail to him, after six months visit,
> The unidentified What-is-it?

> *Samuel Hopkins Adams,*
> *Hotel Klindt, Caracas,*
> *Venezuela.*
> *Thanksgiving 1908*

T he last of the twelve invited guests took his assigned seat at the table for the Thanksgiving gathering in the ornate dining room of the Gran Hotel Klindt on the *Plaza Bolívar.* Samuel Hopkins Adams, the famous muckraking reporter for the *New*

York Sun and *McClure's*, was among the diners. Charles Johnson Post, an artist and an author, was also present. Venezuela was in a bad way, the kind of bad that drew international newspaper correspondents like Adams and Post. The recent antics of Cipriano Castro, the enigmatic dictator of Venezuela, hadn't disappointed them or their editors.

William H. Phelps, a young businessman who had come to make his mark in Venezuela, was at the table along with members of the US legation now out of work since President Theodore Roosevelt had severed diplomatic relations with Venezuela only months before.

All of the diners were men. All but one lived as bachelors in Venezuela. If they were married, their wives had long ago deserted them and returned to the comfort and safety of the United States. Only the wife of the Reverend Theodore S. Pond, who, like her husband was a missionary of long standing in Venezuela, withstood the rigors of the land to minister to the poor. The reverend was at the dinner. His wife was not. Except for Henry Tom, the British vice consul, all of the diners were US citizens.

The first diner to take his seat was Cyrus N. Clark, a recent arrival to the country. It was Reverend Pond who had introduced him around the city as an attorney from New York representing wealthy capitalists in the northeastern United States. Pond made sure to explain that Clark and his family had been longtime friends of the Ponds back in New York.

Clark sat between Adams and Post. He'd made sure of that. He lived in a spacious guest room on the second floor of the Klindt. A walkway overlooked the gilded atrium-style dining room. When he stepped from his room to the walkway to come down to dinner, he glanced over the banister to see if the members of the wait staff had prepared the table as he'd instructed them to. He grimaced. Something was wrong.

After quickly descending the wide staircase to the first floor, he entered the dining room, brushing past an older man who was greeting patrons as they entered. Trying to be inconspicuous, he walked directly to his table.

Personalized place mats announced where each guest was supposed to sit. Someone had been there before him. He scanned the room quickly, using the eight large Venetian mirrors on the walls to see if anyone in his party was present. Deciding not, he began fussing with the place mats, assuring that his seat was between Adams and Post. He then sat down to wait for the rest of the party. He felt confident that the two correspondents could help him find an outlet for his own news articles on Venezuela's troubled times. He'd already sold an article on Castro to *The Outlook* the previous August. Its editor, Lymon Abbott, was a former pastor at Plymouth Church, to which his family had belonged in Brooklyn.

Appearing impatient, he motioned for a server. He asked for bourbon with mint, knowing that the hotel didn't stock either. He frowned as he listened to the server's apologies, and then he waved the man away.

He picked up the place mat that was addressed on the cover to Señor Clark. It was four pages. The stanza by Adams was on the second page. It referred to "the deep-conspiring CLARK," with his name hand-printed in red capital letters. A caricature followed on the third page. It had been drawn in color.

It showed a man resembling Clark with a gun and a holster on his hip. He was smoking a huge and ornate pipe. A second gun was sticking out of one of his boots. The face in the caricature was an accurate portrayal. His thick hair was parted down the middle, and his moustache had a slight twist at each end. The pipe was also a regular feature. It was seemingly attached to him like a limb.

Clark was pleased by the way that Adams had portrayed him. His description mirrored exactly the air of mystery that Clark sought to present with his new identity.

The swashbuckling clothes and weapons, however, weren't at all like the high-collar shirts with ties that he always wore under traditional wool suits.

It was natural that Adams' invitation would raise the issue of Clark's purpose in Venezuela at just this time. In hushed conversations, Clark alluded to unnamed men of great wealth who wanted to invest in Venezuela. Men with more experience in this strange land were skeptical of Clark's claims. Conditions couldn't be worse for investment.

Clark had become immersed into Venezuelan politics during his brief months in the country. His astute insights, his confident manner, his impeccable social skills, and his articulate discourse amused and entertained the few Americans residing in Caracas. He also amused the US minister and the British minister whom he'd already befriended. He called on them regularly, seeking their advice about possibilities for business concessions in the country. He asked them to introduce him to government officials. While neither minister was too optimistic, both agreed to do what they could. Clark used the time he spent with them to familiarize himself with the views that their two governments had on Venezuela.

The lyrical reference that Adams made to the length of Clark's visit was off by a month. He'd been in Caracas since the middle of April. He was living in his third residence since leaving New York the previous February. He first landed for a brief visit in San José, the capital of Costa Rica. Then he traveled to Cristóbal in the Canal

Zone. These were places where he believed he knew no one, and no one knew him. While that was the case, neither stop led him to the business concessions that he was seeking. So, he considered Venezuela. He was aware that Pond was there, and he was confident that he could enlist him as an ally and trust him to keep his secret.

La Guaira was the port for Caracas. Before arriving there, Clark had traveled without a passport. When he had sought passage on a Royal Mail Steam Packet Company ship from the Canal Zone, the ticketing agent had informed him that a passport was required to enter Venezuela. It wouldn't be a problem—not then and not later. The ticket agent introduced him to the Venezuelan consul, who drew up a passport in the name of C. N. Clark and then handed it to him.

He'd cleared the port only days before the dictator, Castro, reluctantly ordered a quarantine after conceding that bubonic plague was present.

As with many things, Castro's handling of the plague would have been comical if it had not been so deadly.

The Venezuelan government's first response was to deny that the plague was present in La Guaira. Dr. R. Gómez Peraza was the chief of the Board of Health. He attended the first patients. When he had the audacity to declare that the outbreak was plague, Castro had him jailed.

Understanding the implications of his own diagnosis, a replacement doctor sent down to the port from Caracas ruled out that it was plague, and the Venezuelan Board of Health issued a document declaring that the sanitary condition of La Guaira was perfect.

The board took the unusual step of requiring all foreign consuls in La Guaira to sign a certificate that attested to this. Still, no one believed it. Five hundred stevedores normally worked at the port. They were put to work sanitizing La Guaira. Port business was brought to a standstill, and the steamers carrying goods for Caracas were diverted to Puerto Cabello on the north coast, where their loads were then transported to Caracas by way of a German-owned railroad. The spiraling costs of the additional transportation had driven the price of flour to twenty-five dollars per barrel. The plague was costing the government hundreds of thousands of dollars in customs revenues.

In his first dispatch to the State Department about the health conditions, the US minister requested that a warship be sent to Puerto Cabello. If Caracas and La Guaira became isolated, this would allow them to continue to communicate. His account explained how helpless Venezuelan medical officials were. They were completely unable to deal with the situation.

"I am of the opinion that no one here knows anything about the treatment of the plague, and as quarantine laws are not enforced strictly, and as the gravity of the situation is not appreciated, we may have a very serious time."

In the ensuing months, the plague had spread. Residents of Caracas, which was more than twenty miles from the port, were dying.

The unrelenting ringing of the cathedral bells announced the deaths. It resonated through the capital throughout the day and night. The cathedral was situated diagonally across an intersection from the Klindt. The ringing had become a main source of conversation among the mostly American and European residents and guests. The bells were waking them up at all hours. A small delegation of hotel guests asked the manager to appeal to church officials, but the manager was worried that the archbishop might take umbrage.

Among those who approached the manager, Clark personally volunteered to call on the archbishop to plead on their behalf. The manager tried to dissuade him, but he was outnumbered. Seeking a compromise, Clark got both sides to agree to support a letter, which Clark would draft and sign. In the letter, they would inform the archbishop of their complaints.

Over a period of weeks, one letter turned into several letters. The manager stiffly resisted and watered down each letter. Clark later informed the residents that he had made progress with the archbishop. He had advised him to recognize the deaths at specific times of the day and suspend the ringing of bells at night. The Klindt's guests were pleased with the results.

The plague was one in a series of problems that Castro had badly mishandled. Rebellions, murder of opponents, and his own wasteful lifestyle led to differences with his own people and other nations, leading to Roosevelt's suspension of relations. Beyond the various international squabbles, Castro's enemies inside the country were growing. His health was seriously deteriorating, and the country's economy appeared beyond repair.

The gathering was on the Saturday following Thanksgiving. In recent years, the US legation had hosted Thanksgiving for the US colony and some members of the government of Venezuela. This year, with the legation house closed, no one had considered celebrating. The dinner at the Klindt had been hastily assembled to discuss the epochal events that had occurred only days before and those that were imminent.

For several weeks, rumors of revolution swept through Caracas, feeding anxious fears of violence. Then, on the Monday preceding the gathering at the Klindt, Castro issued an announcement that "Peculiar circumstances compel me to go to Europe for a short time."

Castro was ill with colovesical fistula for which he badly needed surgery that Venezuelan doctors would not dare to attempt. He sailed the next day.

Left in charge of the country was the vice president, General Juan Vicente Gómez. Everyone was certain that revolution was at hand.

For the US legation, certain issues needed to be immediately clarified. Washington was already looking for guidance, and the legation's evaluation would guide its superiors back home.

If government leaders couldn't settle quickly on a replacement, was there a risk of armed conflict? What kind of man was the vice president? Did he have the support to take over the country? Presuming the US president would want relations to be restored, how long after that would it take to reopen the legation?

The question of relations being renewed was further complicated. In January, the United States would have a new president. William Howard Taft had won the election and was only months from inauguration.

Before dinner, the conversations over cocktails began in urgent, whispered tones. As the realization settled in that Castro was gone and he would never return, the discussions became louder and almost gleeful. They now saw a possibility for a new beginning with a workable diplomacy without the lies and the wild gyrations of Castro.

After scotch, they ordered wine with dinner. When the time came for port, cigars were broken out and passed around. Everyone but Pond and Clark lit a cigar. Clark didn't have his favorite tobaccos from the United States, but he made do by borrowing some South American tobacco and smoking it in his pipe. Pond didn't smoke.

The importance of the moment wasn't lost on the wait staff or the other diners. They no longer had to fear Castro or treat him with false pretenses of respect. Long ago, disgust for the dictator had spread throughout Venezuela and far beyond.

People disliked him on three continents. Astonishingly, a solution had appeared.

It was late in the evening and the drinks had taken their toll. The diners rose to leave. The United States and British legations, which at times were competitive, frequently found common ground on the important matters. Castro should never return. That was the message that the legation sent back to Washington. Tom attended the dinner so he could reliably inform the British minister of the advice the US legation was sending the State Department. In the days following the dinner, the fears of violence subsided. Caracas grew giddy with anticipation.

Gómez feigned loyalty to Castro for twenty-five days. Confident that he would succeed, he seized power.

Ever since the rupture in relations, Washington had been using Brazil to represent US interests in Venezuela. The two countries communicated through the Brazilian embassy in Washington. A week before Christmas, official word from Brazil reached Washington. The dispatch read:

"Reaction initiated against General Castro. Minister for foreign affairs saw me today; asked make it known [to] American government wish [of] President Gómez to settle satisfactorily all international questions. Thinks convenient presence American warship La Guaira in prevision of events. He [Gómez] made similar communications to [other] legations. Please transmit Rio."

The Venezuelan foreign minister had also informed others within the diplomatic community of Gómez's intention and suggested to several legations, including the British, Italian, and United States, that they should send warships. Ostensibly, the ships would be present to protect their citizens in the country should violence break out. The foreign minister felt that warships from these countries would warn any opponents of the coup against taking any action. And, it would prevent the Dutch from reacting, since their position toward Venezuela was becoming increasingly aggressive.

Roosevelt responded immediately by sending a signal of approval.

The United States sent several ships, including the *North Carolina*. Aboard this ship was a special commissioner named William Buchanan. He was carrying instructions to confer with the Venezuelan government to reestablish diplomatic relations. He also planned to obtain a statement from Venezuela committing it to the arbitration of American claims against it. The claims were associated with damages suffered by US citizens from the revolutions during Castro's reign.

Accompanying Buchanan was William Tecumseh Sherman Doyle of the US State Department. He went by W. T. S. Doyle. He was an attorney who was born in Menlo Park, California. Doyle first visited Venezuela in 1903 with the North American Mixed Commission, which considered the claims of European nations regarding the earlier blockade of Venezuela.

Doyle and Buchanan took residence at the Hotel Klindt. The US legation informed Clark of their imminent arrival. Clark met them at the door of the Klindt and introduced them to the owners. The next morning, he bumped into them in the reception area on the first floor. He discovered that they were trying to have breakfast but couldn't locate anyone to take their order. Clark explained that breakfast was served in the rooms, and he summoned a waiter from the kitchen.

Before he left, Clark informed them that he was well known to the US legation. He implied that he could possibly be of assistance to them in their mission, adding that several Venezuelan government officials were his good friends.

Clark didn't know it at the time, but meeting Doyle was providential. The man would become his closest friend. Although he was younger than Clark, Doyle would be his mentor. Doyle would never, however, learn about Clark's real name or his past.

The State Department immediately began sizing up Venezuela's new strongman. The early reports that were circulating in Washington were positive. After all, the man welcomed US warships into the harbor and promised to negotiate debt claims.

The US minister informed Washington that he had found the new president, the man who would become known as the Tyrant of the Andes, "a man of good intentions." Everyone agreed that Gómez would be better for Venezuela than Castro. That was also the conclusion in Washington, both at the State Department and the White House. But so very little was known about the man.

Buchanan, now working for President Taft, moved quickly. The accord was signed in early February. In early March, the United States reestablished formal relations with Venezuela. Meanwhile, Gómez was making other international strides. All the while, he was cementing his power inside the country. The outside world rejoiced that Castro was gone. Most nations viewed his replacement as much more desirable.

The US press responded quickly, too, no doubt guided by the positive position taken by the State Department. In its Christmas Eve edition, the *New York Times* had reported on Buchanan's trip to Caracas with great enthusiasm. According to one article, "The civilized governments of the world welcomed quietly the departure of Castro."

In addition to establishing US warships in the harbor and renewing relations, the United States provided further support for the new government by ordering the US Navy to actively track Castro's international travels. The United States aimed to ensure that he wouldn't reenter Venezuela on a filibustering expedition. The urgency of the tracking efforts would occasionally spawn simultaneous Castro sightings on different continents. The United States also pressured Great Britain, Holland, and France to bar Castro from their shores. Many Venezuelans would later look back upon this time and wonder how the United States had been naïve enough to support Gómez so strongly.

Clark was quick to notice the changes. He believed that there was new possibility to win a contract to clear the great sandbar at the entrance to the harbor at Lake Maracaibo. He was fixated on the project. By charging tolls on the ships entering and departing the harbor, he felt certain that they would generate profits.

His efforts to penetrate Castro's government had been futile. Government officials had been too fearful of the dictator to approach him on Clark's behalf, and Castro was wary of outsiders. He was particularly wary of people he called "concession hunters." The new dictator appeared to be open to the United States. There was new hope, and just in time. Clark needed money to survive. And there were wealthy friends in New York willing to consider investing in Venezuela. One, in fact, already had advanced money to Clark to escape the United States and seek a new life with his new identity.

3

RETURN TO THE SCENE OF THE CRIME

O f all places in the world, New York City was where Snow ran the highest risk of being exposed and arrested.

He'd lived in Brooklyn for all his life. He'd spent two decades working as an attorney. He'd had offices on Wall Street, and he'd been a high-profile president and chairman of one of the city's most respected universities. His name had appeared in countless newspaper articles. Some of these articles documented his battles with Mayor Seth Low over the running of the city's libraries. His face had appeared on the front pages of the same newspapers as an embezzler who was on the run.

The risks didn't faze Clark.

If he were to have a chance encounter, he'd talk his way through it. He'd shrug off the allegations by blaming the newspapers and the district attorney's office for shoddy reporting and investigating.

He'd claim that the district attorney had withdrawn all charges against him. He'd explain that after the district attorney had personally apologized, he'd decided to let the matter drop. He hadn't even demanded retractions from the newspapers. He'd shrug and say he just wanted it all to be behind him.

He knew it would work. He'd spent his life charming people, winning them over, and making them accept whatever he said. He'd practiced his delivery. He'd practiced the words that he would say, the way that he would act, and the facial expressions that he would make.

The police hadn't been able to catch him months before when they were trying to apprehend him. He had no evidence that they were even actively pursuing him.

He considered it more likely that he'd bump into a former associate, or perhaps a neighbor.

Besides, he had no choice. He was nearly broke and New York was the one place where he had wealthy and loyal friends, including George Marshall Allen. Allen was a book publisher and yachting enthusiast who had given Snow money as he prepared to escape from the country.

He traveled home on the steamship *Zulia* of the Red D Line, which was the primary transportation service between the United States and Venezuela. The Dallett family of Philadelphia owned the line. The ship flew a white flag with a large red "D" in the center.

The line's four steamships ran two routes carrying cargo, mail, and passengers from Brooklyn to various stops in Venezuela and the islands in the Caribbean.

The *Zulia* stopped at ports in New York, San Juan, and Curacao. In Venezuela, it stopped in La Guaira, the port that served Caracas, and Puerto Cabello on the north coast of the country. It returned to New York via Curacao and San Juan.

The ship was comfortable. It was two hundred sixty-six feet long, and it was capable of traveling at twelve knots. The steamer had two masts. It was equipped to carry thirty-five passengers in its first-class staterooms. As many as twenty-four other passengers could stay in less glamorous cabins. Common lavatories were under the poop deck. The fare was ninety dollars.

As was the case with most ships during this time period, the crew on this trip vastly outnumbered the eight passengers who were going to New York. An Englishman who was about Clark's age boarded with Clark at La Guaira, along with a young Argentine husband and wife who resided in Caracas. A young American woman who was traveling alone was the fifth passenger to board the ship at La Guaira. Among three passengers boarding at Curacao was Albert Morawetz, the US consul-general-at-large.

Between long meals that were served in the ship's dining room, the passengers spent their time strolling along the promenades. Clark knew none of the passengers before the ship had embarked. As always, he played the enthusiastic bon vivant while he was aboard. He was especially charming when he was playing bridge in the ship's smoking room with Morawetz, his new consul-general-at-large friend. Bridge was the primary form of entertainment on board.

His name was listed as Cyrus N. Clark on the ship's manifest. His place of residence in the United States was left blank.

The steamer left La Guaira on August 9, 1909. It arrived in New York on August 16. He'd been away from New York since February 1908. His peaceful family life as Henry Sanger Snow seemed to have existed a long time ago. He knew there was no way to reverse the path that he'd chosen. He didn't dwell on it.

He always assumed that he would take trips back to New York. He harbored two concerns about it.

His first concern involved his family. Anna and the children would expect to see him, and that would be dangerous if police were watching her. When Anna informed him in a letter that she was taking the children to Europe for education, he knew that the time was right.

Now the only concern was arrival.

The *Zulia* docked at Pier 11 in Brooklyn. He didn't dare spend time there. It was too close to his former neighbors and the telephone building at 81 Willoughby Street in Brooklyn Heights where he'd committed the embezzlement.

Allen retained an apartment on Broadway, but he resided at his mansion estate in New Jersey. He was pleased to allow his friend to stay at his apartment. Since he had disappeared, Clark had been using the address as a postal drop.

The apartment was located at a safe distance from Clark's old neighborhoods in Brooklyn Heights and Wall Street.

Meanwhile, Anna and the children were living a simpler life supported by her own benefactor.

Andrew Carnegie's involvement with Anna's father dated back to 1850. Her father was David Brooks, a telegrapher and a colleague of Samuel Morse.

Playing a game of draughts one day with Carnegie's Uncle Hogan, Brooks asked the uncle if he knew of a young man who could work as a messenger in his telegraph office in Pittsburgh. The uncle mentioned Carnegie. Carnegie was then seventeen years old. He was working as a bobbin boy in a cotton factory in Allegheny City.

The young man jumped at the chance. He later wrote, "And that is how in 1850 I got my first real start in life. From the dark cellar running a steam engine at two dollars a week, begrimed with coal dirt, without a trace of the elevating influences of life, I was lifted into paradise, yes, heaven, as it seemed to me."

When Brooks died in 1891, Carnegie seemed to have lost his opportunity to repay what he viewed as a significant debt.

Carnegie got one more chance when the Snow family's pastor approached him in 1908 and asked him for financial help. Henry Snow needed money to pay back the companies he had stolen from.

Carnegie said no.

Within days, he wrote to Dr. Newell D. Hillis of Plymouth Church in Brooklyn:

"This affair had for me a bad beginning, as you know, and I had to refuse to be a party to paying the creditors. The cloud now has a silver lining. Perhaps you will go with me someday to see the heroine, who exalts human nature. I have had hundreds, yes, hundreds of cases for my pension list, but while there have been many splendid revelations of human nature, I feel this morning that Mrs. Snow excels all—truly heroic."

Carnegie sent two checks for three thousand dollars to help Anna pay for immediate expenses. Shortly thereafter, he gave her a gift of twenty-five thousand dollars and an annuity in steel bonds that would produce three thousand dollars a year in ongoing income. He also paid to educate her children.

Still, the period of transition had been difficult on Anna and the children.

Despite Carnegie's aid, the family's financial condition hadn't permitted them to remain at their beautiful home on Henry Street with their four servants. Anna first moved the family to smaller quarters on nearby Joralemon Street.

Their circumstances turned worse when Constance, the youngest child, was set upon by neighborhood boys who taunted her calling her father a thief. A fistfight ensued. Then Anna received a written threat from someone signing the letter as the "Black Hand" and attempting to extort money from Anna, and threatening to kidnap Constance.

Concerned, Anna reported the letter to the police. She was worried that her family was vulnerable, and she concluded that her family would be safer in Switzerland.

For Clark, it was the beginning of a period of frustrating stops and starts. The turmoil that his family had been experiencing, which he learned about in letters from Anna passed to him secretly by friends, aggravated him. Events controlled his life. He was not in control.

Despite promises from Gómez personally for two massive government projects, no contract had been forthcoming. When Clark tried to follow up with other government officials, they shrugged, making vague comments that "El Jefe," which was sometimes used to refer to Gómez, must have changed his mind.

Concluding that he alone couldn't pry anything out of the dictator, he sought a partner for his projects.

While he was in Caracas, Clark introduced himself to Grant Hugh Browne of Flint & Company. Based out of New York, this company had been active in Venezuela for several years.

Clark hoped that Flint's previous work in Venezuela would sway Gómez to award him the project for removing the Maracaibo bar.

Within days of arriving in New York, Clark followed Browne's suggestion to call at his country estate in Goshen, which was north of New York City.

He tried to sell Browne on the project.

Browne patiently heard him out, but he had other ideas. He asked Clark if he was willing to go back to Caracas to negotiate the purchase of the Imataca iron deposits in the Orinoco Delta on behalf of Flint & Co. Showing no disappointment, Clark quickly expressed his willingness, but he left the estate without having worked out any details. After not hearing from Browne for a while, he worried that the matter was dropped.

Clark explained what then occurred. "I did not again call on him for some days, but when at last I did so, he exclaimed, 'Where have you been? I've been trying to get hold of you. Your passage is taken for return to Venezuela by the next steamer!' He then took me to meet his associates of Messrs. Flint and Company, with whom we discussed fully their wish to acquire the Imataca iron mine, to negotiate for which I was engaged to act for them."

Browne had liked Clark from their first introduction in Caracas. He hired him without conducting a background check. None of the Flint employees in New York identified him from the earlier newspaper photographs.

It had been a short visit home, only six weeks.

Clark sailed south again aboard the *Zulia*. The impostor was up to his old games again. He befriended a passenger who coincidentally was on the same mission for another bidder. The fellow voyager represented one of three groups that were bidding for the mining concession. The third man was a representative for Charles M. Schwab, the successful US industrialist. Schwab had co-founded the Bethlehem Steel Company.

"The loquacious fellow voyager," Clark later wrote, "speedily disclosed that he was going down on the same business as my own, acquisition of the Imataca mine. He showed me his maps and other documents of consequence, which naturally engaged my interest; nevertheless, I did not feel bound to disclose to him the purpose of my own journey!"

Clark was in Caracas for fifteen months. He was no more successful than he had been at winning a concession for himself.

"We were all competitors dickering with the government and learning the true significance of the Spanish word *mañana*," Clark wrote.

The months wore on with incessant delays and postponements. Clark complained about the Venezuelan government and a competing Canadian syndicate, the Canadian-Venezuelan Ore Company Limited. That company was based out of Halifax, Nova Scotia. G. Fred Pearson represented it during the negotiations.

Clark felt that the company had used some sleight of hand to gain the contract for the mines. He described the intrusion of an influential Venezuelan lawyer. This lawyer had prevailed on the attorney general of Venezuelan to issue the competitor a title to the property. The lawyer, whom Clark charged with paying off the government official, then "closed with the Canadian agent and the rest of us abandoned the field."

The conclusion of the Imataca negotiations left Clark unemployed. Once again, he looked to New York.

This time, he sailed aboard the SS *Maracaibo*, departing Curacao for New York on January 26, 1911. This time, he would be in New York for a year. He would reside on 130th Street with a doctor and his wife.

He had another plan to win the harbor concession, but it would take time to nurture.

He turned to the US State Department, believing that it would surely influence Gómez. He'd met a representative of the British Ethelburga Syndicate, which had several concessions in Venezuela already. He convinced the man that Gómez would be more receptive to a joint effort between Britain and the United States. He encouraged him to call at the State Department, where Clark's friend Doyle was the chief of the Latin American Division.

He would also use his friend William Russell, the US minister in Caracas. He would later use Russell's replacement, John W. Garrett. Both of them were recipients of a fierce letter-writing campaign. He warned them that US investments in Venezuela were falling out of favor.

He claimed that his associates in the United States felt that the present government in Venezuela was "consistently opposed to the encouragement of American investment or enterprise in that country and I can hardly blame them."

In his series of letters, Clark complained to the legation that he'd spent two years introducing attractive and legitimate business to Venezuela. He added that he had the backing of American capitalists.

He explained, "In two of those, the Imataca negotiation and the project for construction of the maritime channel at Maracaibo, I had General Gómez's assurances of approval only to have those assurances prove utterly valueless!"

Clark wrote to Doyle from New York in November 1911 to explain his plans. He informed him that his prospective partner was planning to travel to the United States, and he hoped to call on him at the State Department.

He began the letter "My Dear Doyle." His familiar tone in this letter was quite unlike most of his writing. The stationery carried a return address of 45 Broadway, Room 60, New York.

> If I were not of a Christian and forgiving disposition I should simply ignore your very existence, since you are in my debt at least two letters to which I have received no acknowledgement. I am charitable, however, and assume that the

onerous duties of your office are the explanation for your apparent neglect of a quondam friend.

You remember well and pleasantly our very good English friend, Mr. George Williams, of Caracas, in charge there of the interests of the Ethelburga Syndicate of London. Since my first visit to Venezuela, Williams and I have maintained a cordial friendship, which has led us to exchange views upon matters Venezuelan with the greatest freedom, especially relating to the conditions for foreign investment in the country, and the most effective means for so doing.

He told Doyle of their intent to approach the Venezuelan government as part of a mutual partnership between British and US interests.

The difficulties of a purely American enterprise, he said, "have been made very apparent to me in the two large projects which I have presented to the government during the past two years, the purchase of Imataca, for which last summer I offered, on behalf of a syndicate here, four hundred thousand dollars cash and a tonnage royalty; and my Maracaibo maritime channel project, to open up the port and lake of Maracaibo, to do which at our own expense I provided an organization and capital here in New York."

He urged Doyle to agree to meet Williams, assuming Doyle's active involvement could jumpstart the project.

Six days later Doyle received a telegram from Williams, who got his meeting with Doyle at the State Department on Nov. 13 and outlined Ethelburga's operations in Venezuela, which included five navigational projects.

Unfortunately, the fiercest opponent to the removal of the sandbar was General Manuel Antonio Matos. As the minister of foreign affairs, Matos reminded the dictator that if heavy deep-draft tankers could enter the lake, so could the warships of other nations.

There was another reason for rejection of Clark's bid. His proposal did not explain how the work would be done. In his formal application to the Venezuelan government, he had said that the "barra" would be removed by engineering expertise from the United States and a newly developed technology that he labeled "secreto cientifico."

Venezuelan government engineers weren't impressed.

Learning that Clark was back in New York, Browne once again stepped back into his life, asking Clark if he could go to Bogotá, Colombia, on behalf of Flint & Co.

Browne wanted to grow his business in South America, but the outcome of the Imataca negotiations was so vexing that he didn't want to try anything in Venezuela.

He wanted Clark to evaluate whether Colombia offered better opportunities. He was aware that hostility toward the United States still simmered because of the role of the United States in Panama's independence and the building of the canal. These hostilities might prevent a US company from doing business there.

That month, Clark sailed again aboard the SS *Zulia*. Within three weeks, he'd filed a report to Browne, advising him to look elsewhere. Colombia was not receptive to US business developments.

While Clark was in Bogotá, he'd called on the US minister for his views on Colombians' sentiments toward the United States. During the conversation, the minister mentioned the visit to Caracas of US Secretary of State Philander C. Knox. Doyle was traveling with him. The minister was trying to send some papers to Knox.

Clark immediately volunteered to transport the papers, knowing that it would likely lead to an introduction to Knox.

However, when Clark inquired about passage to Caracas, he was shocked to discover that leaving Colombia was going to be much more difficult than arriving.

I had learned before leaving Bogotá that the upper Magdalena River had fallen so low that steamer navigation was impossible. And that I must choose between a two days' journey on the quarter deck of a mule, with another for my baggage, in order to reach Honda on the lower river, or else return to Girarádot, the port for Bogotá, on the upper river, and then descend that stream on a raft.

We were to sail at 11 p.m., when the moon rose, and at that hour the raftsman came to the hotel, shouldered my baggage, and led the way to the river.

The raft was formed of logs bound together, with the smaller ends narrowing toward the front. It was sixteen to eighteen feet long and the rear half was built up a foot or so higher, for the passenger. My baggage was securely fastened at the back of this upper deck, which was floored with strips of bamboo, making a fairly smooth surface.

I disposed myself for sleep thereon, while my navigator took his station at the bows of the ship, armed with a broad-bladed paddle with which to keep the vessel in the middle of the current, which was running swiftly. Two or three times during the night I was conscious that the ship rocked unevenly as we ran a bit of rapid water, but I slept fairly well until morning. Though the lower river is full of ferocious alligators, there are none in the upper stream, so that I undressed several times during the day and swam alongside my ship.

We reached Ambalema in the evening after an enjoyable voyage, the only exciting incident of which was the passage of the Jaramillas Rapids, where the waves soused me from head to foot, necessitating undressing to dry my clothes in the sun.

After spending the night in a small *posada Ambalena*, Clark caught a train for Honda the next morning.

There I passed another night and on the next day went by train to La Dorada and boarded the good ship *Cordelia* for Barranquilla, Colombia.

The river was so low that the down-river trip took eight days. The steamer frequently grounded on some sand bank, when the crew would go overboard and heave in harmony with the engine to get her off.

After a wait of three days at Barranquilla, I sailed on the French steamship *Guadeloupe*.

On the voyage, I bethought me that I might have difficulty landing for during my year in New York I had published quite a diatribe against General

Matos, the Venezuelan minister for Foreign Affairs, whom I considered chiefly responsible for the denial of a contract I had been seeking for construction of a deep-sea channel at the port of Maracaibo Lake.

With this apprehension I went ashore when the ship called at Puerto Cabello and wired the American delegation at Caracas that I was on the *Guadeloupe* with dispatches for the secretary of state.

The wisdom of this precaution was apparent when we arrived at La Guaira on the following morning.

A government collector met Clark at the port. He carried a dispatch from Matos. Matos had instructed the collector to avoid customs regulations, frequently an onerous procedure at the port, and to deliver Clark to the railway station. Clark took the early train to Caracas.

At Caracas, he was whisked through the port with the papers for Knox as a special favor for the United States. Waiting for him was an invitation to a reception and ball at Miraflores Palace.

Clark decided to retain the papers and hand them over to the secretary at the reception. This would guarantee that he would meet the secretary. His acquaintances at the State Department now included the head of the Latin American Division, the secretary of state, and the former and present US ministers at Caracas.

He would have to find a way to take advantage of his new friends.

4

OUR MAN IN LA GUAIRA

Thomas Voetter, American consul at La Guaira, was an un-inspired man, plodding through his day-to-day chores hunched over his typewriter, dispatching the bureaucratic paper-work that was always stacked on his desk.

He avoided more challenging work and whenever possible personal contact. He also avoided writing reports on Venezuelan political conditions for the department back in Washington. He could have gained attention by providing his superiors with skilled analysis about what was going on inside the Venezuelan government, but Voetter feared that only the worst could come from being noticed.

August Leefmans was his vice and deputy consul. With Leefmans also living at La Guaira, Voetter was able to pass off the most onerous work to Leefmans. He was especially inclined to give Leefmans those interminable queries from companies back home. These companies would often ask about business opportu-nities in the country. The queries often contained vivid descrip-tions of a nation that was quite unlike the real Venezuela of the early 1900s. The people who wrote these letters would imagine

43

bustling roadways filled with cars. They would imagine a coastline that had been made safe for shipping by legions of lighthouses. They would envision hospitals with the latest in surgical instruments.

What documents Voetter couldn't pass off to Leefmans, he placed in the top drawer of his desk where they resided for years as space allowed. Leefmans always took what he was assigned without complaint. This included walking daily from the consulate at No. 7 Calle del Leon to the port. He would cross the highway to do battle with the local customs bureaucracy, or he would examine the wares that the steamships were importing or exporting. The citizens of La Guaira rarely saw Voetter. He seldom left the consulate, which was also his residence.

When Leefmans was at the dock, visitors to the consulate found themselves frequently ignored by Voetter. The consul wouldn't look up. He would only acknowledge people with a grunt. Even those who walked across the colorfully tiled floor to Voetter's desk couldn't catch his attention when they were standing directly in front of him. When he would finally look up, he would imply through his mannerisms that the visitors were bothering him. Voetter preferred not to have visitors. He was completely devoid of social niceties, and he was armed with a disapproving demeanor. He instilled resentment within the Venezuelan and American communities.

Leefmans had been at his post for three years, since 1909, and the consul was pleased with the man and his work. With his quiet manner, the vice consul never upstaged Voetter.

His sudden death was a shock.

Saddened, Voetter informed the State Department:

La Guaira, Venezuela, November 8, 1912
The Honorable
The Secretary of State,
Washington
Sir:

I have the honor to inform you that August Leefmans, vice and deputy consul at this place, died last night from a disease of the heart. It is with much regret that I transmit this news, for Mr. Leefmans was a conscientious, faithful, and efficient consular officer, and much of the success that may have attended the work of consuls at La Guaira in the past has been due to his able and loyal services.

The American outpost served as the port for Caracas. It was located twenty-two winding miles down the mountain from the city. It was a busy consulate. It coaxed and cajoled Americans, their interests, and wares into and out of the country. Voetter needed help and he needed it soon. Without help, he'd be forced to take on personally the daily chores at the dock.

Four days later, Voetter wrote to Washington again. He was loathe to inform the State Department that he'd found a replacement for Leefmans. The replacement would carry the title of a mere clerk. The official notification listed C. N. Clark's starting date of service as November 11, 1912. Voetter made it clear that he wasn't enthusiastic about his choice.

"He is the only American citizen that I know is free for employment in this section."

Months before Clark's appointment, the relationship between Clark and Voetter had begun badly. On the trips back and forth between New York and Venezuela, Clark had developed a friendship with Captain Alfred W. Pressey of the *Zulia*. Pressey was Clark's favorite captain, and the *Zulia* was his ship of choice. While he was in New York, Clark had arranged for friends to smuggle his favorite American tobaccos to him on a regular schedule.

In September, Voetter made one of his rare appearances at the dock. He stumbled upon Clark's scheme when he boarded the *Zulia* after it had landed. Captain Pressey approached Voetter immediately, assuming the consul was there to pick up the tins of tobacco for Clark.

Voetter refused the tins, huffily calling them contraband.

Upon returning to the La Guaira consulate, Voetter informed the US consular agent at Caracas to tell Clark "his package is floating around the seas somewhere."

Voetter went on to reveal receipt of contraband of his own, telling the agent, Richard Biggs, that all he could manage, with his limited powers, was to receive a small crock of butter for himself each month, delivered by a steward from one of the vessels in port.

Clark didn't let the matter drop. Biggs sent a hand-written note to Voetter the next week. He told Voetter that Clark had been asking about his tobacco. Biggs instructed Voetter to contact Pressey when the *Zulia* was next in port and obtain the tins. If there were a cost, Biggs stated, Biggs would cover it with funds from the Caracas legation. Voetter wasn't pleased but he followed the instructions.

Voetter disliked Clark and he sensed Clark's scorn for him. The consul couldn't understand why others liked the man. The smuggling incident and its outcome left the consul feeling deeply distrustful of Clark. He was on alert for any transgressions. He feared that Clark must have some connection at the legation. Perhaps he was a friend of the minister.

His wariness was evident in his official notification of Clark's appointment as clerk at the consulate. It was the first of many times that Voetter would point out that Clark had engaged in efforts to win concessions in Venezuela on behalf of American capitalists. His view was that the efforts excluded the consideration of Clark as a permanent replacement for Leefmans.

"He can for at least two or three months and probably for a longer period give his services as clerk at this consulate."

Shortly thereafter, Voetter became ill. He was forced to rely totally on Clark. He became so weak that he was confined to bed, and he had to ask Clark to dictate a letter to the State Department. In the letter, Voetter stated that Clark was being promoted to vice and deputy consul.

"The reason for this nomination is that I am suffering from an attack of yellow fever," Voetter said, "and do not desire the work of the consulate to be interrupted."

Clark recalled his hiring fondly.

"In November of the year 1912, the American consul at La Guaira asked me if I could come down to the port and assist him in the work of the consulate, his vice consul having died. I was glad to do so, as in addition to the pay, which was, I think, one hundred twenty-five dollars per month, it would not interfere with my press correspondence nor with my efforts to secure commercial representations. The consul's illness threw all the work of the office, which was a busy one, on my shoulders, certifications of invoices, preparing bills of health for the steamships, examination and disinfection of hides, and the consular correspondence, before I had time to familiarize myself with the duties."

For many consuls in remote posts, the choices for assistants, clerks, messengers, and vice consuls were limited. In some cases, a professionally educated and professionally trained officer might be assigned from Washington. However, local officers in many consulates were left to make do with local talent.

Sometimes, they had to hire people who were not Americans. Leefmans was a native of Curacao. Voetter's lack of diplomatic options was evident in the case of the vice and deputy consul at Puerto Cabello. A year earlier, the American consul had to inform the legation at Caracas that Venezuelan authorities had arrested his vice and deputy consul after he had taken two shots at one of the natives. The diplomatic breach had occurred on Christmas Day at four o'clock in the afternoon. The vice consul, L. J. Verhelst, was intoxicated when he pulled a revolver from his pocket and shot at a Colonel Páez, who was one of the commanders at the port.

The consul reported, "Mr. Verhelst was arrested, placed in jail, and kept there for twenty hours. I suspended him immediately and have recommended to the Department of State that he be discharged at once from employment of the government."

In recent years, the US legations at Caracas and La Guaira had been fortunate enough to have reliable support personnel. Although the presence of the United States in the country was limited, various men had agreed to serve. This included Clark's friend, Rudolf Dolge. Dolge had come to Venezuela to improve his health. Doctors had told him that he hadn't long to live. He served as consular agent at Caracas for several years. An American named John Brewer replaced him. Brewer had been in the service for years. Several years before Clark's arrival, William Phelps worked as the vice consul.

Verhelst's appointment was not the only one that went wrong, however. A Briton named Benjamin George Pengelly had to be terminated when a small scandal surfaced. Pengelly was attempting to extort payments from a company that was treating hides in Caracas. Pengelly was charging exporters a higher fee per hide than he was supposed to. Half of this fee usually went to the US agent overseeing the process.

Clark was educated, articulate, and popular. With his enthusiasm and high energy, he was a godsend to everyone around the docks but Voetter. With efficiency and flourish, Clark took on the day-to-day routine of the port and the nearby office. He kept the State Department back home apprised of his efforts. He also updated them on Voetter's health. Clark's ever-present civility and good cheer were noticed immediately as marked improvements to the dour, expressionless consul.

Clark now had a full-time job. He found it necessary to move to La Guaira. He gave up what everyone considered a far better lifestyle in Caracas, which had clubs for men and less humid weather. The round-trip commute would have taken four hours out of his day. The train tracks curved up and down the ravines between the city and the town. The train seemed to barely hold its grip around the twisting curves of the mountain's face. Fortunately, La Guaira had a hotel. The Neptuno provided permanent quarters for people who wanted them. Clark was one of these people.

Clark had been as cautious with his consulate employment application as he would later be with his US citizenship and passport forms. He was very cautious in dealing with his new life and his new identity. The application listed the date of his birth as May 8, 1856, and it listed the location as New York City. Henry Sanger Snow shared this birthdate and this hometown. He indicated that he was married and that he had four children. He listed Doyle, who worked at the State Department, as the person who had vouched for him.

Of his education, he wrote, "Private schools, tutors in United States and abroad." This information would be hard to trace, even if the State Department bothered to do so. However, it didn't bother. Clark also indicated that he was in perfect health. He said that he could speak and write Spanish and French, and he had some knowledge of German. He was honest about his birth, his marriage, his parents, and his wife's name. He was honest about the names, ages, birthplaces, and birth dates of his children. All of this information was exact and truthful. The only exception was the name Clark.

The job application also inquired about his occupation. He wrote, "Engaged for my own account, and in association with friends in New York and this country, in the investigation of properties for investment, negotiation of contracts, etc."

By December 10, Voetter was busy trying to wash his hands of Clark. He sent a misleading dispatch to the department crediting Clark's actual appointment as having been done by another officer, the *chargé d'affaires* ad interim at Caracas. He added that the appointment had been an emergency.

"At this time, I would state that I do not recommend that the appointment of Mr. Clark be considered as other than a temporary and emergency character, principally for the reasons set forth in the last paragraph of my No. 101, of November 12, 1912, and if the department can make the appointment of a suitable person to come from the United States soon I would be pleased."

While the job didn't pay much, Voetter added, perhaps a young man with an interest in learning consular work might find it attractive. He mentioned a Mr. Digneo of Santa Fe, New Mexico. He'd recently been in contact with him. When the State Department investigated Digneo, it discovered that he was not yet twenty-one years old. This was a requirement for the post.

The New Year passed and still there was no replacement. Voetter had requested a replacement before the spring. He hoped to take leave then, and he wanted someone in place who had received some training before he departed.

March came and Voetter went ahead with his leave, ceasing active duties on March 23. The next day, Clark's dispatch to the department acknowledged that Voetter was absent from his post.

Voetter was on leave for three months. The indicted embezzler-turned-vice-consul was in charge of US interests at the port. In addition to normal consul duties, US officials asked Clark to make extensive translations for the government of the United States. The documents that he translated ranged from paperwork involving Venezuela sanitary code, legal proceedings against the former dictator Castro, and new laws on trade, banking, and copyright. He was turning out to be much more useful to the legation at Caracas than Voetter had been.

5

MINISTER MCGOODWIN

When Woodrow Wilson, the new Democratic president in Washington, nominated Preston Buford McGoodwin in 1913 to become the US minister to Venezuela, he ran into opposition from the start. Members of both parties in the US Congress had their doubts. His nomination was almost withdrawn in the Senate, where Democrats questioned his party credentials. Republicans lined up in opposition. They said that he was unfit for office.

McGoodwin was a former newspaper editor. He had been born in Princeton, Kentucky, but at the time of his nomination he resided in Oklahoma. The Democratic opponents claimed that he had done publicity work for presidential candidate William Howard Taft, a Republican, in the recent campaign.

The *Washington Post* put it another way. "Strong opposition to Preston McGoodwin of Oklahoma has developed because of his alleged unstable Democracy."

The *New York Times* reported that McGoodwin had worked as private secretary to a Republican congressman, and it claimed that he had been the editor of two Republican newspapers. It, too, also alluded to the report that he had done publicity work in the Taft campaign prior to the Republican convention.

The cacophony from Congress should have been a warning of the trouble that always swirled around McGoodwin, but President Wilson eventually got his way.

In choosing ministerial nominations, Secretary of State William Jennings Bryan made certain that the Democrats from the South received their share of the spoils that the new administration was handing out. Bryan's letter to Wilson in May 1913 explained that the Venezuelan mission would soon be vacant. Its minister, Elliott Northcott, was leaving. Bryan laid out the batting order for the president.

"If Gonzales is selected from South Carolina, Hale from North Carolina, McMillin from Tennessee, Lamar from Florida, and Leavell from Mississippi, a number of the Southern states will be taken care of. You already have some Virginians in mind. I think that McGoodwin of Oklahoma is the man from that state, and I would like to consult with the senators from Arkansas in regard to a man from Arkansas."

The president was anxious to get the new man to Caracas. He had just been informed that Castro, the former Venezuelan president, had just landed in Venezuela with an army.

Although it was widely circulated, the report eventually proved false.

In a letter, the president introduced McGoodwin to the Venezuelan government. He spoke of McGoodwin's "high character and ability."

Along with McGoodwin's commission, Bryan included a letter to McGoodwin informing him that his annual salary was ten thousand dollars. He also explained that the contingent expenses of the legation were not to exceed three thousand dollars a year.

Bryan also approved the hiring of a clerk with an annual salary of one thousand eight hundred dollars.

Bryan concluded his letter by saying, "Entire confidence is entertained that the affairs of the legation will prosper at your hands, and that the ties which have so long united the government of Venezuela with that of the United States will be strengthened, if possible, during your incumbency."

The first reports about the new minister were positive. A commission that had just returned from the country informed Bryan that McGoodwin and his wife, Jean Curtice McGoodwin, were "standing well with the people down there." Bryan conveyed this information to President Wilson.

The British legation, however, wasn't so impressed. The first official assessment mentioned his arrival in October. The legation said that he was a journalist from Oklahoma who "likes it to be known that he originated from Kentucky." It put his age at thirty-four, but it expressed the opinion that he looked "far older."

The critique continued in its somewhat imperious tone.

"He exemplifies the saying, 'once a journalist always a journalist.' In the first two or three weeks of his arrival he wrote thrice to the local press, signing himself 'yours fraternally,' on matters he had not communicated to the Venezuelan government. He is serious, agreeable, and unobtrusive to the point of dullness in his intercourse with other people, but his wife makes him entertain frequently."

The British opinion of McGoodwin didn't improve with amplification. The British minister in Caracas, Frederic D. Harford, explained a few things about the McGoodwins to the Foreign Office. They were intimate with Dr. José Gil Fortoul. Fortoul was an intellectual and a supporter of Gómez. He had held many positions in the government over a long period of time. McGoodwin's relationship with Fortoul was viewed as embarrassing, and it didn't increase his prestige. His prestige was also not improved "by his somewhat lavish entertaining, due to adroit flattery by a small clique of society who wished to amuse themselves at his expense."

The British minister chortled that McGoodwin was the only minister in Caracas who had sent his congratulations to Gómez on the anniversary of the downfall of Castro.

He also informed London that McGoodwin "does not go out anywhere, breakfasts at 1:30 p.m., and goes to bed at 1:30 a.m."

Clark's relationship with the new minister had a friendly beginning. However, Clark had been unable to control his propensity for whispering campaigns and rumor mongering, and he had mocked the minister behind his back.

When the McGoodwins took their first vacation home to the United States, an incident aboard the ship brought great derision from the small US colony in Venezuela when it learned about it. The front-page account in the *Puerto Rico Progress* detailed a confrontation over the possession of two staterooms.

When a copy of the newspaper reached Clark, he couldn't resist from spreading the news through the US communities in Caracas and La Guaira. The incident erupted into a full-fledged protest against McGoodwin's behavior. Lionel M. Parker labeled McGoodwin's conduct as "unbecoming a gentleman." Parker's wife had been a victim of the McGoodwins.

Parker had reserved staterooms aboard the SS *Caracas* for his ailing wife and their children. They would be traveling from San Juan to New York. When the steamer arrived in San Juan from Caracas, the McGoodwins were occupying Parker's rooms. They refused to surrender them.

The ship's purser informed McGoodwin that his passage called for a change of staterooms at San Juan. McGoodwin responded by saying that H. L. Boulton had personally promised him that he would have these quarters all the way to New York. Boulton was the Venezuelan agent for the Red D Shipping Line. The purser called the ship's captain.

He, too, informed McGoodwin that Mrs. Parker and her children were scheduled to occupy the rooms when the ship reached San Juan. He noted that Mrs. Parker had been ill for a long time, and she was traveling north on account of her health.

McGoodwin's response was described as more "forceful than diplomatic." He was overheard telling the captain "he'd like to see the color of the man's hair who was going to put him out."

The captain summoned representatives of the Red D Line. They came aboard but they "were unable to budge the minister and his family."

The situation was resolved only when Mrs. Parker capitulated. She agreed to take other quarters. Other passengers had been drawn into the fracas, and they had agreed to double up so that a suite would be available for Mrs. Parker and her children.

Parker's hand-written complaint to the State Department said that after the ship set sail, McGoodwin had told other passengers that his own son was "only just recovering from a serious illness, and he could not be expected to relinquish the room in question."

Parker exposed the statement as a lie.

"Mrs. Parker has the assurance [of the physician of the S.S. *Caracas*] that Mrs. McGoodwin presented a certificate on boarding the ship stating that the boy had fully recovered, and that [the doctor] had examined him and found him well and perfectly fit."

McGoodwin wrote a response to the State Department, and he included a letter from his wife. In his own version, McGoodwin denied ever having seen or spoken with Mrs. Parker.

He claimed that he had not been on the ship when the incident had occurred. Mrs. Parker, he claimed, had accosted Mrs. McGoodwin, demanding their quarters. He said that she had "openly and grossly insulted" Mrs. McGoodwin as she did so. McGoodwin said that other passengers had given Mrs. Parker two staterooms to pacify her. He said that her newly assigned rooms were on the side of the ship that was "more desirable" than the side where the McGoodwins were staying. To bolster his case, McGoodwin enclosed a cabin plan for the ship.

In Mrs. McGoodwin's letter, she claimed that at the time she had not yet fully recovered from a case of pneumonia. She said that her son "was stricken with typhoid fever in severe form."

In the accounts that the McGoodwins gave, the ship's doctor attended to the boy throughout the trip. Mrs. McGoodwin said that the doctor had warned her to restrain the boy's movements while he was aboard the ship. He had made these recommendations for health reasons.

Although he came to know that Clark was responsible for spreading the salacious details among the US colony, McGoodwin uncharacteristically overlooked it. He saw something of himself in Clark. He noticed the similarities in their duplicitous natures.

Besides, he learned quickly that Clark possessed a natural ability to understand Venezuelan politics. Clark's contacts within the Venezuelan government proved beneficial to McGoodwin. As a minister, he had no diplomatic experience and he was new to the country.

In fact, McGoodwin was enthusiastic and lavish in his praise for the vice and deputy consul at La Guaira, and he frequently mentioned Clark in his dispatches to Washington.

As McGoodwin tried to find his diplomatic footing, the fledging US administration was trying to find its own place in

Venezuela. With the changeover from Castro to Gómez, its early dispatches to McGoodwin were unsophisticated, unrealistic, and too supportive too early of Gómez.

One cable from Bryan instructed McGoodwin to confer with Gómez on the possibility of a revolution. "Ascertain the causes of same and see whether they can be removed," Bryan instructed him.

He also asked McGoodwin to obtain a statement from Gómez on when he would hold elections. Bryan wasn't done. He wanted a full report on the characteristics of probable revolutionary leaders. He wanted to know whether the "revolutionary spirit" was spreading or decreasing in Venezuela.

The maneuverings of the wily Venezuelan president presented an impossible test for McGoodwin. Washington regularly pressed him to seek out the dictator and see what could be done to help him.

McGoodwin was reticent about calling on the dictator. Most of their communications were done through third parties in the Venezuelan government.

Eventually, Washington's early hopes turned into concern. Clark and the British minister had schooled McGoodwin. By the middle of 1914, McGoodwin had begun to grasp the situation, and he was informing the State Department about the real situation in Venezuela.

He noted the drafting of a new constitution from the constitution that had been revised in 1909.

The minister outlined the changes, and these changes left no doubts about where the government of Venezuela was heading.

Beginning in April 1915, the presidential term was to be lengthened from four to seven years. The prohibition of the incumbent's reelection was eliminated. Gómez also abolished the

Office of the Vice President and the Council of Government. He also awarded himself the command of the army. In the event of his own absence or disability, a cabinet member of his choice would act temporarily in the Office of the President.

The older Latin hands at the State Department had watched Gómez for five years, and their opinion of him dropped with each year.

The Latin America Division at the State Department conceded by then that they were to blame for Gómez's rise to power and his continued reign. In November, Charles Lyon Chandler and Rutherford Bingham of the Latin America Division examined the possibility of affecting a change in leadership.

Chandler acknowledged that the United States was responsible for events in Venezuela, while criticizing the continued "unconstitutional methods" employed by Gómez.

"It seems to me we must be very careful about handling Gómez," Chandler wrote. "We were morally, if not more so, responsible for putting him in there."

Despite all of Gómez's faults, Chandler wondered whether he still "may not be better than some weak creature either without any stamina as [General Francisco] Linares Alcántara or with a bunny-rabbit mind as old [Antonio] Guzmán Blanco had in his last days."

Chandler's view was that "moderate soft shell despotism" was needed in the country. "If we insist too much on maintenance of the strict letter of the constitution, Venezuela has had more of these since 1810 than in other country in the world, it will make a bad impression in other Latin American countries; they will think we are going too fast and too far, too much interfering with sovereign state, etc. So we had better let Gómez stew in his own fat.

Anything that happens there must come about as a result of his own doings, not as coming in any way from us."

Chandler suggested that someone should instruct McGoodwin to approach Gómez discreetly to inform him that the United States couldn't recognize any government that had come to power violently. McGoodwin should tell Gómez that if he stepped aside, "no bones will be broken and no harm done." Then Chandler said, "We must see that someone gets to be manager who can really develop the country."

Washington wasn't getting it. Gómez had already suspended the constitution. A trusted confidante was serving as the provisional president and Gómez, as chief of the army, was surrounded by his most trusted forces at his home away from home in Maracay. His opposition lived in the three political prisons or in exile. Gómez wasn't going anywhere.

In a cable to the State Department in April regarding the Castro Revolution that reportedly had broken out, McGoodwin said that Gómez had fabricated the revolution as an excuse to continue to stay in power and suspend all rights.

McGoodwin had watched silently as Gómez dismissed his Council of Government after it took exception to the president's position on the French Protocols. This agreement allowed French citizens to settle financial claims against Venezuela. Gómez found a more pliant group of men for the council.

The full annual report from the British minister in Caracas to the British foreign minister, Sir Edward Grey, summarized the major events of 1913 in Venezuela. These included, in the British view, Venezuela's renewal of relations with France, suspended since January 1906, and the fabricated Castro Revolution, which was now viewed by other nations as having never occurred. It, however, had been used by Gómez to hand the presidency over to Dr. Gil Fortoul. Gómez then took on the role of the commander of the army.

That done, Gómez then was off with his army to Maracay in early August and did not return until early January of 1914 with a "triumphal entry" into Caracas not having fired a shot in anger.

The small uprising at Coro in July 1913 in which Castro wasn't physically involved had been encouraged by local authorities who were loyal to Gómez. They had assured the invading forces that the population would rise up in support of the invasion, British minister Harford wrote. Instead, Gómez's troops immediately swept up and arrested the invaders.

The scheme was put into place by Gómez. General León Jurado, a close friend of Gómez and the president of the State of Falcon, in which Coro was located, did as he was ordered. It was his waiting battalion which seized the invaders.

Several weeks later, in what Harford called a "comic opera," a gunboat arrived at Coro to launch a few cannon rounds at the mountain there. This gesture was meant to convince citizens that a serious battle was happening. It was meant to justify Gómez's "taking to the field" in search of a revolution that didn't exist. The British like others concluded that Castro had never been in the country.

Overwhelmed by these events, McGoodwin was being viewed alternately with amusement and distrust by State Department personnel. His seesaw relationship with Gómez was too fawning early on. But now the State Department was beginning to cool to Gómez.

McGoodwin's behavior was also being called into question.

The US legation offices were being used as a venue for late night drinking and poker. This was also being viewed with distain with the British legation particularly critical.

Chameleon, meanwhile, was enjoying himself. More knowledgeable, articulate, and facile than consul Voetter, his frequent dispatches to the minister on the political machinations inside Venezuela made him popular with McGoodwin.

6

GREAT ESCAPE I

C lark's patience and cheerfulness with Venezuelan customs officials added to his good reputation with the legation in Caracas. He responded with a smile to the pettiness of minor Venezuelan officials and the onerous regulations that they enforced. His respectful familiarity with the officials helped him avoid eruptions over tariffs, passport seizures, and illegal contraband. It also gave him direct access to his tobacco, which arrived regularly from North America.

La Guaira wasn't a favorable posting for American diplomats. Over the years, it had taken its criticism from the US legation staff. Everything was a target. The US legation staff had criticized its weather, its poor health conditions, and its lack of culture and entertainment.

La Guaira had once been considered Venezuela's most important post. It handled all of the trade and all of the travelers going into and out of Caracas. State Department professionals, however, had come to know it as a way station where one languished until something better came along. Few State Department professionals wanted to work in La Guaira. It wasn't unusual that an

American with some language skills and no obvious employment would represent the United States there. They would have hired somebody who was not from America, as long as he spoke the language.

An ode to La Guaira was published in March 1908 in *The Pan American Union*. In this ode, La Guaira was called "the most maligned port of all South America."

In an article titled "La Guaira the Picturesque," a gentleman arrived in La Guaira from the United States. Immediately after disembarking, the storyline went, he began running after a train that was departing for Caracas. The American had been instructed to avoid the heat at La Guaira at all costs, and he'd taken the warning to heart.

The writer stated that "Many people live in La Guaira all their lives, and I know a number who are not dead yet."

The writer described La Guaira as the principal port of northern Venezuela. The writer said that it was the port of "ingress and egress for the capital, Caracas, the 'Paris of South America,' with which it is connected with a wonderfully scenic and picturesque railway."

The port's bustling trade was expansive. The writer said that it averaged twenty international ships per month. The slowest days saw fifteen to twenty small sloops and schooners bringing in or exiting with cargo from other coastal towns or nearby islands.

At the one hundredth anniversary of the official presence of the United States at La Guaira—it opened an office for the first time in January 1833—an enterprising legation member, Ben C. Mathews, distributed a lengthy publication entitled, *The First Hundred Years Are the Hardest*. He dedicated it to "those officers who are dissatisfied with their posts."

This irreverent collection of materials began with a poem of remembrance and farewell. Winfield C. Bird, a former consul, had written the poem. He had survived for nine years, eight months, and twenty-six [or eight] days at the post between 1881 and 1891. Once he'd withdrawn from his position and was safely at sea, his poem called "Adios La Guaira," was distributed, He became legendary around the distant American outposts of American influence in the world.

One stanza read:

"Farewell ye gloomy *casas*, major *dicho* prison cells,
Ye dirty crooked *calles*, reeking with assorted smells;
Ye dirty little coffee shops, ye filthy *pulperías*,
Stinking stables, dirty patios, and fetid *cañerías*."

Mathews, writing in the consulate records, pointed out that there was little to choose from for entertainment. However, it wasn't an especially dangerous post. Only one US consul had developed yellow fever. It was Voetter and he survived. Furthermore, only one consul had been shot at. A Venezuelan soldier had fired and missed the consul. Unfortunately, the bullet hit his wife and caused a minor wound.

This was the history, the present day, and the future of the place that the impostor found himself calling home.

He was an American who needed a place to get lost in, and Venezuela provided this refuge. The US colony was small and visitors from the United States were infrequent. This reduced his risk of coming face to face with someone who could expose him. No one had shown an inordinate amount of interest in his background.

Steamships offered the only regular transportation to Venezuela from the United States. Most communications reached Venezuela slowly. US newspapers arrived well after publication.

The Venezuelan government had little capacity or interest in vetting foreign arrivals. It chose to focus its investigative and spying efforts on its citizens within Venezuela and exiled communities outside of the country.

Immediately after Clark's first arrival, bubonic plague had caused the nation's ports to be quarantined. Yellow fever led to his promotion from clerk to vice and deputy consul. These were not the only health threats. Typhoid, malaria, smallpox, tuberculosis, and amoebic dysentery all flourished.

Leprosy was also prevalent. Venezuela's new leprosy hospital opened in La Guaira the summer before Clark first appeared. This hospital replaced an aging and decrepit facility at Caracas. In the early hours of June 20, 1907, the English railway transported one hundred and ten patients in open freight cars to the new facility. Once they were unloaded, the train cars returned to the rail station at Caracas, where they were set afire.

Despite the threats, so far Clark was enjoying good health.

In the course of his duties, he became familiar with Benjamin George Pengelly, the chief accountant and the assistant manager of La Guaira Harbor Corp., Ltd. This British corporation owned and ran the port works. It was natural for them to meet and become friends. Pengelly was a Briton who had preceded Clark as vice consul in the US consulate at La Guaira. In 1907, he was forced to resign after an inquiry determined that he had been extorting gratuities. He had been receiving extra money for inspecting animal hides that were going into and out of the country. The purpose of the inspection was to assure the absence of contagious disease.

Venezuelan shippers were required to have hides inspected before they were exported. They paid a fee to the inspectors, who were frequently vice consuls, for each hide. The US consul at La Guaira investigated Pengelly. The investigation indicated that the practice of exporters paying vice consuls was routine. The consul determined that the minister at the time was aware of the payments. Gratuities above these fees were forbidden. The investigation ruled that Pengelly had been applying pressure on shippers to pay him more money. He was soon out of work.

Pengelly and Clark had more than their consulate jobs in common. They also shared accounting backgrounds. As with Clark, accounting caused Pengelly's undoing. It fell to Clark to ignore all perils and to step in to save the Englishman. Why he took the risk isn't known. His own explanation was a lie.

Pengelly was born in the Greenwich section of London in 1875. His parents raised him and four other siblings. His father was a sail maker. Pengelly started work as a clerk for the Salvation Army. In 1901 he was still living with his parents. At twenty-six years of age, he became an accountant. In December of that year, he married Emma Ann Thomas, and they moved to Venezuela. By the summer of 1906, Pengelly was working for the US legation.

By 1912, Pengelly had taken a job with the La Guaira port works company. In October he traveled to the United States for the first time. His reason for the trip was to purchase a handgun. He returned to La Guaira aboard the *Coppername*, which stopped at Trinidad and then went on to La Guaira, where his wife awaited him. He traveled with a servant.

Pengelly told Clark that he had gone to New York to purchase the gun on the orders of his boss. His boss was Henry Duncan Lewis McDougall, the managing director of the port works. McDougall eventually died by that gun.

Clark's account of the incident years later absolved Pengelly of wrongdoing. Clark knew better.

In December 1912, we had a tragic happening at the port. Mr. Pengelly, chief assistant to the manager of the British corporation which operated the port works, accidentally shot and killed the manager. Pengelly was an amiable chap, the friend of everybody with whom he dealt and always ready to do a favor; in short, one to whom the commission of a crime of the sort was unthinkable.

He had procured while in New York an automatic pistol, at the manager's request, and was in the act of explaining its operation when the gun exploded, he having omitted to remove the last cartridge from the firing chamber.

The examining magistrate who heard all the evidence and examined the witnesses, including the Public Health Surgeon, and myself, completely exonerated Pengelly as to the crime, but sentenced him to one year of prison for careless handling of a dangerous weapon. He took appeal, but was sent to Caracas as a prisoner.

While there, he became quite ill and was transferred to the city hospital, where he remained under surveillance and in nominal confinement for more than a year.

Meanwhile, his enemies, mainly Englishwomen of Caracas whose virtue had been shocked by certain irregularities in Pengelly's life, supported the authorities of the Harbor Corporation in the prosecution of the criminal appeal. Their efforts succeeded in getting him sentenced to twelve years on the crime! From this, he again appealed, but a few close friends, convinced that he might lose the appeal and that a long imprisonment would be fatal, studied the possibility of an escape.

Two doctors in charge of the hospital, who likewise had been convinced of his innocence, asked me if I would cooperate in a plan for his release, which I willingly agreed to do.

Pengelly had improved so much that he was able to walk with two canes in the hospital grounds, and was even allowed to visit the home of some nearby friends, where he enjoyed music.

I was still living at La Guaira in May 1914. While at the friends' house, Pengelly had been fitted to a trunk, with a rounded top, from one end of which his friends cut out a piece of the wood and replaced it with a fine wire screen similarly painted.

On an agreed morning, when I gave notice that the Red D ship *Maracaibo* was in port, whose chief steward was Pengelly's warm friend, he took a walk in the grounds. Observing that no one was in sight, he climbed into the tonneau of a waiting motorcar and into the trunk which happened to be there. Off went the car to La Guaira to my hotel, at whose rear entrance was an occupied room which I had engaged. The trunk was taken into this, "to unpack and rearrange its contents," as I told the proprietor. The "contents" got out and lay on the bed until I gave notice in the early afternoon that it was time to repack, when he again got into it and was loaded on a cart for transport to the wharf.

The escape had gone smoothly. Once they reached the port, though, things went awry.

Clark explained his rising concerns. Pengelly's trunk lay for two hours on a flat car beside the ship, along with other baggage that was destined for Curacao. Fortunately, the hand-made respirator kept Pengelly alive by assisting him with his breathing.

However, the police had a higher than normal presence at the port. The doctor who had the keys to the trunk and a boarding ticket for Pengelly panicked. As he fled, he handed the keys and the ticket to Clark.

> With no little difficulty, I located the trunk and got a couple of roustabouts to haul it out and put it in the cargo sling from the lower deck cabin which I had secured. I went aboard and directed my men until it was deposited in the cabin.

Clark dismissed the men and immediately locked the door to the cabin behind them. Quite concerned, he walked quickly back to the box and leaned over it.

> Pengelly, are you there? I heard a low reply and, fearful that I should find our man in a state of col-lapse, dead, or dying, I cut the ropes which had been used for added security, unlocked the trunk and threw it open.
>
> I found our friend doubled up, as he'd been obliged to lie, in his underclothes and with great beads of sweat on his brow. Grasping him under the arms, I heaved him into a lower berth and

hurried to the steward for a tumbler of brandy and water.

With this, I revived him and adjured him to lie quiet until after the ship should sail, when the steward would look after him.

All went off as arranged. The steward cared for him, and the next morning, after all Curacao passengers had left the ship, got him clandestinely ashore in a barge, and he was taken care of by friends until a ship came along bound for England.

Shortly thereafter, Clark received a letter from Pengelly. It was dated June 2, 1914.

My dear Clark:

I really have to apologize to you for being such a bother over my luggage, but I was hoping it would have been possible to send it to me in Curacao.

However, I am away from there homeward bound, and I have only one change of clothes, one pair of shoes, and one hat. Thank you for small mercies.

If you possibly can, do please forward baggage to Henniker & Hogge Ltd, Southampton, as 'Ropa Usada,' and it will reach me safely.

I do not want to lose it, if it can be avoided.

Again thanking you with all my heart for all your kindness.

Believe me,
Very sincerely

The letter was signed "B. G. P." Under the signature, Clark typed, "From Benj. Pengelly, who affected a sensational escape from Venezuela!"

Clark blamed Pengelly's plight on the Englishwomen who disapproved of his lifestyle or were his rejected lovers. This was of course a fantasy.

Long before Clark wrote about this incident, a true depiction of the incident was revealed.

The information of the death of its manager at La Guaira arrived by cable at the corporation headquarters in London on December 10. It was four days after the shooting. Major Frederick Montgomerie Carleton was another one of the firm's directors. He was dispatched to La Guaira to take charge until another full-time replacement for the dead man could be appointed.

The company's regular annual report of revenues was released in late April. In the body of its report, the real story emerged.

The document contained a revenue report and a description of the friction that was developing between the corporation and the La Guaira and Caracas Railway, which the corporation sought to purchase. There was also an acknowledgement that the previous year had been "one of trial and stress for the directors. In the first place, the board was deeply shocked when, on December 10th, it received cable advices of the death of their managing director in La Guaira, Mr. McDougall, owing to a revolver shot, and that Mr. Pengelly, the chief accountant and assistant manager, had been arrested pending inquiries."

After noting the dispatch of Carleton, the report said, "The board greatly regretted to have to announce that grave irregularities had been discovered in the accountant's department, and that considerable defalcations, extending over some length of time, were being traced, but whatever loss might have been sustained had already been borne by the corporation through the nonreceipt of harbor dues." The report went on to note that the future revenues of the company wouldn't be affected.

A few days after the escape, the secretary of the prefect invited Clark to a lunch. Gómez was demanding to know how Pengelly had escaped.

The secretary raised the subject with Clark.

With some arrogance, the secretary stated, "I can tell you one thing. He never got away through the port. We keep so close a watch over all passengers that no one can get by us!"

Clark inquired, "Don Federico, how do you think he got away?"

His reply, as Clark wrote it, was "I believe he took an automobile to Puerto Cabello and got aboard some ship leaving that port."

Clark responded, "That seems to me a reasonable explanation." If Gómez had confirmed that the escape had occurred at La Guaira, the secretary would have been held responsible. The secretary didn't want that to happen, so he didn't press Clark any further.

In his account, Clark never mentioned the reports of the accounting irregularities.

The shooting death of McDougall was announced in *The Times* of London on April 29, 1913.

The event couldn't have been ignored around the port. Clark's various accounts of his life were usually accurate and frequently corroborated by other records. This included the accuracy of his account in helping Pengelly escape. However, Clark couldn't share the real circumstances about Pengelly's imprisonment with his family. Thus was created the fanciful tale of the five-foot-six-inch Lothario. Perhaps it was Pengelly's dark blue eyes that the women fell for. His extracurricular activities had so shocked the virtues of the good Englishwomen of Caracas that they successfully conspired in a South American dictatorship to have him accused, re-tried and resentenced to a twelve-year sentence for a crime that was much more serious than that which he was originally tried and convicted. There would be more crime in Pengelly's future.

7

THE CONSUL'S TREACHERY

Voetter's numerous attempts to prod the State Department to find someone to replace Clark weren't being acted on and the consul began to look for someone on his own, occasionally suggesting candidates to the department. He would recommend men he had heard about from friends in the United States or from letters he had received from applicants. He used every contact to remind the department that he'd never considered Clark a permanent choice, repeatedly citing his view that Clark's efforts to win concessions from the Venezuelan government disqualified him from long-term employment at the consulate. Others in the legation or in Washington didn't share this view.

Voetter's real problem with Clark was the man's arrogance. Clark considered himself superior to the consul, and he let it show. Clark enjoyed the popularity that he had with merchants, collectors, and customs officials around the port, and he insinuated that this made Voetter jealous, describing him as "no mixer."

Clark had never considered that the consul would dare to fire him. He assumed that his associates, including McGoodwin, would never allow it. However, conspiracies with the regime's enemies in exile were unacceptable to the US State Department, and they were dangerous for those suspected by Venezuelan authorities.

Clark hadn't let that stop him. The year before, Voetter had caught Clark passing money and mail to steamship captains and pursers, who would smuggle them to exiles in Curacao. However, the consul withheld the information from the department at the time. He was worried that he might be held responsible for Clark's actions.

Then a new incident occurred. It involved the once distinguished General Francisco Linares Alcántara, who was now out of favor with the Gómez regime. Voetter decided that it was more dangerous to allow Clark to continue his activities than it was for Voetter to have hidden Clark's previous abuses from Washington.

Regardless of whether or not the situation was awkward, Voetter decided that this time he would use this information against Clark. His explanation of his own actions was clumsy, and it strained credulity.

He told the department that he had withheld information to protect the reputation of the Consular Service. He cited that a written report of such incidents might fall into the hands of the Venezuelan government and be "put to use against an American citizen." That, he said, could lead to restrictions in other necessary consulate activities, such as the boarding of vessels in the harbors.

Voetter expressed concern that if the infractions continued, eventually Venezuelan authorities would discover them. He claimed that Clark's ongoing illegal activities now presented more risk than the likelihood of written reports falling into Venezuelan government hands. He referred to General Alcántara as a "pronounced revolutionist."

Voetter explained what he called the "circumstances surrounding the actions of American officials in facilitating the forwarding of letters to a Venezuelan revolutionist from Caracas to Curacao under the protection of the seal of the American legation." He also explained that someone "who had been granted permission to go aboard for other legitimate purposes" had made arrangements at La Guaira to take the letters onboard a steamer.

The consul then had the difficult task of explaining that it was he who took the letters aboard the ship after accepting them from Dr. Stewart.

"I am confident that it was not the desire of Mr. Clark or Dr. Stewart that I should know anything about this, but as by accident it was given to me to take aboard so the scheme was discovered. I regret very much my not looking at the letters before starting from the consulate, as by so doing the delivery of this letter would have been prevented. I wish to state at this time that I do not consider that Dr. Stewart used any initiative or had any desire to be a party to this scheme of forwarding clandestine correspondence, but has acted altogether at the request of Mr. Clark."

Dr. Stewart was also based at the consulate in La Guaira. He added to the daily dramas there, gossiping with Clark about Voetter and joining Clark in plots to embarrass the consul.

He was a portly man with graying hair and a moustache, and he wore three-piece suits and bow ties, despite the tropical climate. The doctor looked like a theater actor playing Dr. Watson to Clark's Holmes.

On several occasions, Stewart had taken the blame for Clark's missteps with his superiors in the legation and at the State Department. Stewart was as naturally conspiratorial as Clark. They would become good friends.

Voetter's latest shipboard incident was not reported until months after the incident. Voetter told McGoodwin that an employee at the consulate had informed him that Dr. Stewart wanted two letters to be taken aboard the steamship *Zulia*. Voetter carried them with other documents aboard the ship. As he handed them to the purser, he noticed that one of the letters was addressed to Alcántara.

Although the purser didn't want to take it, he did. Voetter said that neither of them considered at that point the possibility that the consul might take back the letter before he left the ship. After a conversation later with Stewart, the consul concluded that Stewart hadn't intended to give him the letters.

His dispatch to McGoodwin was intended to cover himself with the State Department by reminding McGoodwin that Clark had previously passed other mail covertly to Dutch ship captains. He noted that Voetter had twice discussed the infractions with McGoodwin at the time.

He said that those letters went to relatives of Castro, the former dictator, and all of this occurred shortly after the so-called Castro Revolution of 1913.

Given the recent mail violation, Voetter moved quickly, silently, and without warning to remove Clark. He did not even notify McGoodwin.

The reaction to Clark's firing was a firestorm. It was immediate and one-sided. The legation and the US community in La Guaira and Caracas were astonished by what they viewed as Voetter's sudden and improper action.

The flurry of dispatches began on May 15, 1914. The first came from Phelps, who was highly regarded at the State Department as the preeminent US businessman in Venezuela. His devotion to Venezuela was well known, and his businesses grew simultaneously with his prestige and reputation. He'd known Clark since Clark had first arrived in 1908. Phelps had been a guest at the Thanksgiving dinner that year at the Hotel Klindt.

Addressed to the minister at Caracas, Phelps wrote:

> I have heard that it was the intention of the State Department to appoint another vice consul in La Guaira to supersede Mr. Clark.
>
> This news has been a shock to me both personally and commercially, as I have a high regard for Mr. Clark's ability, loyalty to American interests, and personality.
>
> I am thoroughly convinced that it would be impossible to obtain another man who would be of such service to American exporters, American residents in Venezuela, and the department; because of his great experience in Venezuela and the esteem in which he is held by the Venezuelan authorities.

Phelps called Clark's removal a "distinct loss to American interests."

Years before, Clark's friends had supported him during his evasion of the police in New York. Hoping that his firing could be overturned, Clark was again stirring up support for himself in Venezuela.

Clark's friend Dolge, who was now working for Standard Oil, wrote on behalf of the US colony at Caracas and La Guaira. Each member signed the letter. McGoodwin had become the minister in the fall of 1913. He sent his own letter to Washington. He strongly praised Clark's work with the legation, and he called for his reinstatement.

I have the honor to enclose herewith a communication signed by all private citizens of the United States residing here and also from Mr. W. H. Phelps, the principal American merchant in Venezuela.

I have no hesitation in expressing entire approval of what is said by the members of the American colony. My first knowledge of the matter was gained yesterday when I heard from several American residents that Mr. Clark's successor had been appointed without any advance notice having been received by him.

With my knowledge of Mr. Clark's singular ability and his untiring energies, I am firmly convinced that the welfare of the service in La Guaira demands his retention as vice and deputy consul.

McGoodwin pointed out that Voetter was about to go on leave. His goal was to secure a transfer. McGoodwin added:

Frankly, I must say that the acquaintance Mr. Clark enjoys with government officials and his judgment in dealing with pompous and constantly changing petty officials at the port of La Guaira, as well as his standing at the commercial houses here and at La Guaira, do not suffer by comparison with the consul.

Dolge also cabled Senator Elihu Root, who was a former secretary of state. The Venezuelan government intercepted the cable. It was the government's first notification of Clark's firing. It took notice because it had its own interest in Clark.

SENATOR ROOT
WASHN.
AMERICAN COLONY REQUESTS YOUR
ASSISTANCE
DEPARTMENT ASSURE RETENTION OF
CLARK
VICECONSUL LAGUAIRA CONSIDERED
INVALUABLE
PRESENT JUNCTION MINISTER MCGOODWIN
ADVISED
—RUDOLF DOLGE

Senator Root weighed in immediately and directly with Robert Lansing. He was the counselor at the State Department, and he would later be the secretary of state. It was too late.

Bryan had already told McGoodwin that a reinstatement was impracticable because a replacement had already been hired. Lansing wrote to Root shortly thereafter with the same answer.

The clamor that had been raised was highly unusual for the department, but Voetter had prevailed for the moment. State Department practices gave him final rule over his charges at La Guaira. His victory eventually proved hollow, and it worsened his reputation with his superiors.

Voetter was already feeling the pressure and the intense anger of the Americans in and around Caracas. He was immediately confronted by another crisis at his doorstep. Again, Clark was responsible.

A delegation of officials from the Venezuelan government called on him. It was May 15, 1914. The visit wasn't social.

The officials complained that Clark had intervened deeply into the internal affairs of their country. They warned Voetter that Clark was being investigated. They informed the consul that there had been a burglary down at the docks in December 1912. It had occurred just after Pengelly's arrest. Pengelly's desk had been broken into and the contents had been removed. Clark was suspected as the culprit.

The burglary had been brought to the government's attention now only because it was investigating the recent escape of Pengelly. Because the government hadn't yet acknowledged Pengelly's escape, it did not reveal this information to Voetter.

Two days passed before Voetter drafted a dispatch to inform McGoodwin for the first time about the Venezuelan delegation appearing at the consulate. He used his time to try to learn more about the allegations.

Voetter's and McGoodwin's dispatches to each other were unclear and full of evasions.

Voetter downplayed the diplomatic mail breaches, and he was careful to spare himself any blame for not having reported them to the State Department. He also sought to present his firing of Clark in the best possible light.

> I have the honor to inform you in regard to a statement made to me within two days past in reference to my [former] vice and deputy consul, Mr. C. N. Clark.
>
> The statement was made to me in confidence, but as it concerns a member of the American Consular Service I think you should also be informed.
>
> It was to the effect that the government had instituted some inquiries in regard to Mr. Clark, thinking that he had taken a too active part in the internal

affairs of this country or had acted in such a manner as to arouse suspicion.

Specific inquiries were made regarding his conduct.

Voetter ruled out the possibility that the earlier clandestine mailings, as well as the more recent mail infractions, were the cause of the official inquiry. He declared that there was no way the Venezuelan government could've learned of them.

I am quite sure that the government did not know the facts of which I told you before, of Mr. Clark's action in facilitating the passage of correspondence between persons in Caracas and persons non grata to the government in Curacao, nor of his more recent transmittal of letters to France, so that the suspicions must have been aroused by other acts.

You will readily see that if a consular officer is under suspicion, his usefulness as such is greatly impaired and the coming of his successor at this time may prove to be a fortunate happening for the credit of the service.

Voetter's dispatches suggested that mysterious activities were going on. These activities were more serious than violations involving mail pouches. These activities could have brought grave trouble to the legation.

I have not placed in my correspondence with the department any reference to Mr. Clark's irregular actions in regard to clandestine correspondence, so that with the exception of this letter no statement of such action has so far been made. Any intimation of this to the [Venezuelan] government or proof that their agents could have found would have justified them in immediately withdrawing his exequatur if not more severe action, and any intimation of it to the department would have secured instant dismissal.

The consul was warning McGoodwin that he intended to inform Washington about all of Clark's activities.

His dispatch elicited an even more craftily drafted response from McGoodwin.

Two days after receiving Voetter's account of the visitors calling at the consulate, the minister wrote that he'd acted immediately. He wanted to learn if there was any truth to Voetter's contention that the government harbored suspicions about Clark's activities. He wanted to know if there was any truth to their allegations.

He assured Voetter that neither case was truthful. He also stated that he had absolutely no "personal knowledge" of any wrongdoing that Clark had committed.

Neither man indicated whom they had been in contact within the Venezuelan government. These were implausible omissions.

Oddly, McGoodwin concluded by saying that he understood Voetter's position. He said that he hadn't been surprised to learn of the appointment of a new vice and deputy consul.

Over the next eight weeks, the story of Pengelly's escape slowly crept into the public domain. When Pengelly suddenly disappeared from the hospital grounds, the government's investigation turned up evidence of the burglary at the docks in 1912. They also discovered Clark's involvement. The investigators immediately suspected that Clark had helped Pengelly escape. Fortunately for Clark, they lacked any conclusive proof.

Although Clark's role in the escape became known to several State Department officials, they never informed Voetter about this.

Almost a year later, Voetter's transfer finally came through. He and Clark exchanged letters. In the consul's letter, he complained that he had to call on Venezuelan officials to apologize for Clark's involvement in the burglary at the docks.

8

GREAT ESCAPE II

O nly days after his dismissal by the consul and amid the clamor in the US colony over his firing, Clark was at it again. It was much more dangerous this time.

Pengelly was merely a Briton who had murdered another Briton. This time Clark was planning to free the most feared enemy of the dictator. If he were caught this time, Clark had no diplomatic aegis to fall back on.

General Juan Pablo Peñaloza was a loyal son of Venezuela. He was a military and political leader of unquestioned bravery and integrity. He had earned his military title and his honors through serving his country, and he wore his battle wounds proudly.

Under the rule of General Ignacio Andrade Troconis, the former Venezuelan president, Peñaloza had led the army of Venezuela. He had commanded forces that had defeated Castro after a month of fighting at San Cristobal. He had forced Castro and his revolutionary troops to withdraw.

Castro eventually ousted General Andrade from the presidency. Castro's march into Caracas had forced Peñaloza to flee into exile in Colombia, where he stayed until 1908. Gómez then seized power and invited Peñaloza to return.

Gómez appointed his Council of Government [Consejo de Gobierno] to bring confidence and legitimacy to his presidency. Along with a number of sound appointments, he brought in Peñaloza.

But differences between Gómez and the council surfaced over the so-called French Protocols, and Gómez replaced the council in the spring of 1913. Police constantly watched the dismissed members and their families. They were aware of the intimidation, and they were fearful for their lives. Some of the most prominent people fled the country to Curacao and beyond.

As Gómez's corruption and tyranny worsened, the number of discontented exiles in the Dutch-administered island of Curacao grew. The colony of exiles became the focus of the US legation that was based there.

The "general intentions and plans" of the exiles had gotten "into the air of Curacao," wrote the US consul there, "and it does not take a wireless operator to detect them. General Curacao opinion is that Gómez is to be assassinated."

The consul, Elias Cheney, reported to Washington that he "would not be surprised to hear that they had accomplished their purpose any day."

Cheney described the secretive atmosphere among the refugees in Curacao. This secretiveness was necessary because Gómez had spies everywhere.

"No man here ever talks aloud of Venezuela," Cheney wrote.

But people did talk. They found ways to circumvent Gómez's spy network with their correspondence. When talk of assassinations and coups reached Venezuela, Gómez turned to harsher measures inside his country.

General Alcántara had attended West Point, and he had once been the minister of the Department of the Interior. He felt that his freedom and his life were in jeopardy, so he fled to Curacao in the summer of 1913. In late January 1914, those opposed to Gómez became more vociferous. Alcántara distributed a manifesto in Caracas and other points in Venezuela. He was highly critical of Gómez, charging that he'd begun a "scandalous attempt" to overthrow fundamental law in Venezuela.

Alcántara told the people that he'd stood up to the tyrant for two years. Alcántara said that this led to "my separation from the Ministry of the Interior in April 1912 and subsequently to the persecution of my friends and to the painful situation of espionage and intrigue under which I found myself compelled, out of regard for my personal safety, to leave the country clandestinely."

Numerous exiles had preceded Alcántara. They resided in Curacao, New York, and France. Enemies of the state who didn't flee found themselves in leg irons in one of three prominent prisons. Many of them were tortured and nearly starved. Their families were extorted by their prison guards.

Gómez chose the worst of Venezuelan society to run his prisons, including his cousin, Eustoquio Gómez. Eustoquio was a murderer. The leader had illegally freed him from prison.

The outrages that Gómez and his agents perpetrated upon the indigenous citizenry were unspeakable. They redirected the wealth of the country and its citizens into the pockets of Gómez and his friends and family. The seizures were blatant.

Peñaloza was aware that he was being watched after his dismissal from the government, but he maintained his life in Caracas as normally as he could. He maintained his friendship with Clark, and they played chess almost daily.

He'd come to know the American well over the chessboard. Dr. Demetrio Lossada Díaz frequently joined them. He was a dentist who had attended Penn State University, and he later became the minister to Colombia. Peñaloza trusted both men implicitly. The American came to consider Peñaloza and Lossada Díaz his two closest Venezuelan friends.

Over a game of chess, Peñaloza related the circumstances that had led to his replacement on the council and his fears for his life.

When friends inside the government warned him that he would soon be arrested, the general turned to Clark for help.

Over the course of a few days, Clark met with a few collaborators. Clark and the general scripted the audacious escape, borrowing a route that would require the use of a car, a rail car, and a schooner. These kinds of escapes were becoming routine for the enemies of Gómez.

The general was to disguise himself as a priest. He would wear vestments that Clark supplied. The disguise also was borrowed from those who had already gone into exile.

Clark met the general at the Dolge home in Plaza Panteón. He would have to escape from the city in daylight, and he would have to do so before the guards took up their nightly positions at guard posts on the edge of the Caracas.

Communicating through intermediaries, Peñaloza had contacted Gómez at the seaside resort of Macuto to tell him that he was going to visit the dictator soon to make peace with him.

Peñaloza had no intention of going to Macuto, however. Such a feint, he and Clark hoped, would discourage Gómez from having them tracked or picked up if they were spotted leaving Caracas.

Clark was nervous. The schism between Gómez and Peñaloza ran deep. It was possible that Peñaloza was being watched. The general's alert to Gómez that he was coming to visit could backfire. Clark also feared if he were suspected of aiding Pengelly's escape, he could be under surveillance.

Clark's alarm grew when he arrived at Dolge's home.

As Clark had instructed him to do, the general had put on his vestments, but one of the most recognizable moustaches in all of Caracas remained.

Clark would later write:

> In May 1914, it befell that he was warned by friends in the government that Gómez was only awaiting a favorable opportunity to arrest and imprison him.
>
> This occurred but a few days after I had spirited Pengelly away. General Peñaloza told me the situation affecting himself and asked whether I would be willing to assist him in getting away.

Clark had ordered the license plate of the escape car removed and at 5:30 p.m. it arrived at the door of Dolge's home. Once again, the risk of exposure increased.

> The general and I got in. It was a touring car with the top thrown open, and we sat in the tonneau.

Clark knew that the moustache and the open car rendered the general's disguise useless.

> I told the general to lean back and continue using his handkerchief, whilst I made myself more conspicuous. I had been well known as American vice consul. We drove rapidly and by unfrequented streets to the road leading out of town to the La Guaira Highway. At that time, a guard was posted at the city outlet to inspect persons and

vehicles leaving or entering, but this was not until 6:00 p.m.

We passed the post unnoticed before the guard was installed and drove rapidly down the mountain road until we reached a point close to the rail station at Cantinas. From this place, the railway grade is continuously downhill.

There, we were signaled by a confederate, when the general left my car and concealed himself until dark. At that hour, all trains having ceased to operate, the general mounted a small handcar loaned by the railway company and descended by gravity alone until he reached the outskirts of Maiquetía, on the coast.

There he was protected by friends until midnight, when he embarked in a small boat which put him aboard a waiting vessel, and the next morning he was safe in the Dutch island of Curacao.

After leaving him, I kept on to La Guaira and my hotel, but I thought it prudent to be seen in Caracas on the following morning early to avert suspicion.

To aid me in this, I persuaded Mrs. Stewart to accompany me, and we left in my car soon after daylight, arriving at Mrs. Dolge's home for breakfast.

Writing about the escape four years later, the director of US military intelligence, Roger Welles, added to Clark's account.

How General Peñaloza escaped from Venezuela with the assistance of Dr. C. Norman Clark, a loyal American of Caracas, is noteworthy. No passports, of course, would be granted to Peñaloza, so he very humbly sought permission from General Gómez to have an interview with him at the town on the port where Gómez was staying. Gómez, thinking that Peñaloza wanted to apologize for former difficulties and become one of his supporters, consented to receive him.

This gave Peñaloza the opportunity to leave Caracas with the consent of Gómez, and as soon as he arrived at the coast, he immediately got into a small boat and went to the island of Curacao, where he was out of the jurisdiction of Venezuela.

Gómez was informed of Peñaloza's escape on May 31. The dictator was infuriated that he'd been fooled. McGoodwin reported Peñaloza's escape to the Department of State. He wrote that the successful escape "may indicate a lack of diligence on the part of the authorities."

The dictator's brother, General Juan C. Gómez, was the governor of the Federal District, which included the whole of Caracas. The dictator reprimanded Juan and the prefect of police at Caracas. His "demands for vigilance," McGoodwin informed Washington, resulted in numerous arrests.

All of the exiles at Curacao were under surveillance. Every interested party was watching them. Of all of them, Peñaloza stood out among the US military and civilian delegations in Venezuela. In their view, he was the one who could ignite the Venezuelans and incite them to take to the streets.

McGoodwin informed the State Department that the escape of Peñaloza was significant. "He is unquestionably [the] most influential enemy of Gómez. Intrepid fighter, reputation for honesty; never professional revolutionist. For many months has been shadowed by government."

Immediately after the escape, McGoodwin seemed to have been as informed as Clark was about the details. He also was knowledgeable about the split with Gómez.

McGoodwin's dispatches didn't reveal the sources of his information, but he was able to describe how Peñaloza was disguised as a priest during his getaway from Caracas.

Clark and his accomplices were the only direct sources for that information. McGoodwin didn't have regular contact with the Stewarts, the Dolges, or Peñaloza. It was unlikely that he had heard it from them.

The exile communities were becoming more organized. Money collected in Venezuela went to exiles who had fled. This money went toward supporting the exiles or to purchasing arms and ammunition outside of the country for filibustering missions to overthrow Gómez.

Peñaloza later moved to New York City, where he received monthly payments of support from an exile who was wealthier than he was.

Gómez's forces were intercepting mail that was coming into and out of Venezuela. Other methods for transporting letters had to be found.

Clark had already run afoul of Voetter. He had violated the mail privileges that the diplomatic community enjoyed. Getting caught and fired for his transgressions, he remained undeterred.

During the months of Peñaloza's stay at Curacao, I was entrusted on numerous occasions with monies sent to him by friends at Caracas, once, with two

thousand bolivars in gold. These moneys I forwarded by friends aboard the American steamers.

I had many letters from the general while at
Curacao, and later, from Colombia. These came
written on tissue paper, in the general's fine script,
folded very small and placed in the bottom of a box
of matches. They would be brought to me by some
friend; who would look me up at my club, prof-
fer a cigarette, and courteously hand me his box
of matches, which I would forgetfully put into my
pocket!

In his letter of thanks to Clark for aiding his escape, Pengelly
also informed Clark that the general had arrived in Curacao on
June 1. It was two days later when Cheney wrote from Willemstad
to inform Washington of Peñaloza's landing at Caracas Baai,
Curacao. Caracas Baai was a quarantine station that was seven
miles east of Willemstad. Cheney told Washington that Peñaloza
arrived aboard a small schooner and "immediately came to
town, took rooms at the Gran Hotel, and has remained there quietly since."

In September, four months after the general's escape, Clark
received a matchbox letter from Peñaloza. The letter used only
single initials to refer to some people. In his own case, Peñaloza
signed the letter as Z.

When he knew that people were outside the reach of Gómez,
Peñaloza would use their last names. Peñaloza was responding to a
letter in which Clark had offered to smuggle Peñaloza's mail from
Caracas to New York. Clark indicated that a good friend of his was
about to visit him in Caracas, and he was willing to act as courier.

The always cautious Peñaloza declined the offer, saying that the war in Europe had "completely frozen" the revolutionary movement, and he had nothing worth the risk of communicating.

The general also warned Clark about the method of handling future mailings to him. He informed Clark that the carrier should put a two-cent stamp on the envelope in Curacao and then drop the letter at the post office. He told him to address the letter to the "recommended house." After receiving an earlier letter from Clark, Peñaloza had received a warning, most likely from a postal worker in Curacao who favored anti-Gómez forces.

Peñaloza told Clark that he hadn't gone to Colombia yet, but he would do so in the next two months. It would become a staging area for Peñaloza's attacks into Venezuela. He asked Clark to "let our friend's brother know it."

He smuggled another letter to Clark in a matchbox. In this letter, he thanked Clark for the three letters and the sixteen hundred francs he'd received from him.

"May God compensate F for his helpful and on time service," the general wrote. "I already knew his hardships and I will act accordingly in all that matters to him."

His letter grew even more mysterious. "Until today I did not have reason to distrust L. The affair with G. was already known by another person. A secret kept by three people will leak soon."

Once again, Peñaloza expressed that he was sad that the war in Europe was getting in the way of overthrowing Gómez.

"Over here we have not experienced any change," he wrote, "since the war in Europe made our projects fail. Olivares [General Régulo] has gone to New York. I was informed that he left for Europe recently. Say hello to our friends and comrades, and give to M a big hug." He signed the letter, "Your grateful friend, Z."

Was "M" a reference to McGoodwin? Was Peñaloza thanking this person, the US minister, for aiding his escape? The dangers that enemies of Gómez faced by staying in the country were formidable, but flight also had its risk for anyone caught while trying to get away. The travel itself could also be dangerous.

General Alcántara fled to Curacao. His brothers-in-law, General Manuel Blanco and Dr. Raimundo Andueza, accompanied him. The trip had nearly cost Alcántara his life. He almost drowned in the small boat that carried him to Bonaire.

By July 1, 1914, thirty-five of Venezuela's foremost former officials were at Curacao. Peñaloza was at the top of the list, which Cheney prepared and distributed. They were all under the watchful eyes of the governments of the United States and the Netherlands, as well as the network of spies that was working for Gómez.

In March 1915, someone attempted to assassinate Peñaloza at Curacao. Of the several shots that were fired at Peñaloza, one bullet hit him in the back. It penetrated his shoulder blade, but he quickly recovered.

It was assumed the shooter was hired by Gómez, although the suspect claimed otherwise. The suspect said that he and Peñaloza had argued over a money issue. A second attempted assassination of Peñaloza also failed.

Clark didn't explain why he had taken the risk of helping Peñaloza. The general was a friend and his daily chess partner. He did write that he felt justified because the general had done nothing illegal, and he had a right to leave his country. Clark was motivated by real concern about Peñaloza's safety. Once again, he convinced himself that he could get away with helping a respected enemy of Gómez escape the country.

Clark never addressed whether he knew that he was already being investigated before the Peñaloza escape. He also did not address the reason why he took steps against the dictator after he had made so many efforts to ingratiate himself with him.

May had been a busy month for Clark. It left him jobless once again.

9

ONE MORE CHANCE

There was concern at the State Department that La Guaira was out of control. Officials inside Consular Services were trying to understand what was real and what was concocted. No one could recall a similar uprising occurring in a foreign land among US residents over a personnel change. The complaints had gone all the way to the secretary of state.

Then, immediately afterward, word comes that an officer had been smuggling letters and money to exiles who were intent on overthrowing the Venezuelan dictator. The consul himself unknowingly was involved in one incident.

Now there were new insinuations seeming to report Clark appeared to be involved in the burglary of Pengelly's desk at the docks. This burglary dated all the way back to Pengelly's arrest in December 1912.

Even worse, now new allegations were leaking out, claiming that the US legation at La Guaira had spirited a prisoner out of the country. The former vice consul had obviously gone rogue.

Despite the wild accusations about Clark's activities, legation members, including the minister and the entire American community, supported Clark. They did not support the consul.

It was particularly grating that the consul had been asking for a reassignment for quite some time. Then without a word to the minister, he fired his vice consul and hired a replacement.

In July, only two months after Clark's dismissal, Consular Services dispatched Charles C. Eberhardt, the consul-general-at-large, to inspect the consulate under Voetter's tenure and to learn what had gone on. Eberhardt's inspection lasted from July 21 to 24.

Eberhardt also looked into the Pengelly affair.

It was all Clark could have hoped for.

He wrote letters to Consular Services, and he called on the minister in Caracas, complaining of the way that he had been treated. His letters and those of his friends were getting the desired response.

He knew and liked Eberhardt, who was conducting the investigation. Clark felt that he just might get his job back. There was much to be done. When Clark learned of Eberhardt's mission, he approached several men in the US colony. He thought that Eberhardt would likely interview them. He explained that he knew that he had their support, and he claimed that several of Voetter's insinuations were false and inspired by jealousy.

Clark not only did not fear the attention events were bringing to him, he enjoyed it.

Eberhardt's report was long and marked by damaging criticisms of the consul. His language was very different than the language that most department officers at the time used in evaluations.

The first question on Voetter's inspection form asked, "Does the principal officer [or agent] possess the ability to maintain a high standard of efficiency?"

Eberhardt responded, "By education. Yes. By disposition and temperament he seems limited. He has difficulty getting beyond small things. He is reasonably prompt, but only moderately active and alert, and one has only to talk with local merchants to find that he keeps to himself entirely too much to produce the results that he should."

Eberhardt quickly concluded that Voetter was unfit for the post, and he described a specific scene that he had observed.

> In his treatment of visitors to the office, he has a very unfortunate manner, rather short, abrupt, approaching on the sullen, which is at times taken for intentional rudeness. Only yesterday, a caller at the office greeted him on entering, the officer being busy at the typewriter. He grunted recognition, without even turning from his work, left the caller standing, and it was fully two minutes before he even had the courtesy to ask the visitor to be seated.

After five minutes, Eberhardt reported, Voetter turned his attention to the visitor.

> His conversation and attitude hardly indicate insubordination or disloyalty to the department, except as his apparent lack of interest in the verbal suggestions of the inspector [and probably similar lack of interest in what the inspector may write] may be so construed.

Another question on the evaluation form asked about the agent's attitude in interpreting and enforcing instructions.

> He has little difficulty in properly interpreting instructions, but he uses his own will about their enforcement.

For instance, he stopped the use of the rubber stamp as to the accuracy of carbon copies of correspondence because he thought it a foolish and unnecessary requirement. He made no entry in the Miscellaneous Record Book of the recent visit of our battleship *Kansas* because he thought this an old-fashioned and foolish idea.

As to his cooperation with me during the inspection, I may say that beyond the expressions referred to above, and others of a similar nature his attitude was to a certain extent negative, in that he evinced little interest in what I had to say, and when his special attention was called to different items, he received the suggestions with indifference and a don't-care attitude which was a disagreeable surprise to me.

Eberhardt interviewed local residents of La Guaira, members of the US colony around Caracas, and legation members. He quickly discerned that Voetter was unpopular with Venezuelans, noting, "He does not stand well with the local merchants, who seem to feel that he considers himself too good to mix with them at all."

The fortieth question instructed the inspector to "mention strong points in the administration of this office and special features which might advantageously be generally adopted."

Eberhardt wrote, "There are none."

Almost everyone Eberhardt interviewed had negative opinions of Voetter and positive opinions of Clark. Eberhardt sought out Clark.

Mr. Clark was the active, wide-awake member of the office force who affably met and accommodated nearly every visiting American, even though he may have been but a casual traveler through the port. Few knew Mr. Voetter at all, and such as did call at the office were usually treated respectfully but coldly by him.

Naturally, Mr. Clark became much the more popular with natives as well as foreigners, and I am not prepared to contradict the statements of many that it was largely on account of this popularity that Mr. Clark's removal was finally recommended by Mr. Voetter.

I beg to say that I consider Mr. Clark to be the person best qualified as vice and deputy consul at La Guaira in event of a change being made.

Eberhardt was aware that Voetter wanted a transfer and that in his absence Clark could be given another chance.

The accusation that Clark broke into Pengelly's desk shortly after the murder was particularly disturbing to Clark, and he denied it vehemently. He knew that the Venezuelan government had discussed the allegation with Voetter. Apparently, they did not mention that Pengelly's recent escape was the real reason for their visit to the consulate.

As the burglary was the only thing the government had to tie Clark to Pengelly, and by extension to the Pengelly escape, Clark saw it as the most damaging allegation standing in the way of his reinstatement.

After Voetter accused him of the burglary, Clark wrote the consul.

> Before I left the consulate, you deliberately charged me with having broken into Mr. Pengelly's desk in the offices of the Harbor Corporation, in December 1912, and taken papers therefrom, and you said you felt obliged to go in person and apologize for the acts of my vice consul!

Voetter related this information to Eberhardt, who then questioned Voetter about his reasons for firing Clark. Voetter suggested that the Venezuelan delegation that had called on the consulate had implied that Clark's activities involved Pengelly. By the time of the post inspection, the revelation that Pengelly had escaped was circulating. Voetter, it appeared, remained unaware that Pengelly had escaped.

Eberhardt knew Pengelly. In an attempt to confirm Clark's role, Eberhardt asked Clark if he knew how Pengelly had escaped. Clark cheerfully related the story to him. Clark quoted Eberhardt's response.

Eberhardt said, according to Clark, "Good! I'm glad you had the good red blood in your veins to put that through!"

Consular Services shared Eberhardt's conclusion that the differences between Voetter and Clark resulted from jealousy on Voetter's part.

Clark, meanwhile, wasn't without work for long. In late October, McGoodwin hired him at Caracas, informing the State Department that Clark had consented to serve as the consular agent while the present agent took leave. McGoodwin noted that Voetter had been informed. McGoodwin used the opportunity to again throw support behind Clark. When the consular agent returned in March 1915, however, Voetter had hired a replacement for Clark at La Guaira, and the legation had to let Clark go.

In the interim, Voetter's new man landed with a thud. He had been transferred against his will from Trinidad, where he'd been recently demoted. By August, the new vice consul was writing lengthy letters to Eberhardt, whom he'd met only the month before during the post inspection. In these letters, he detailed his suffering at the hands of the State Department.

Edward Cipriani assessed his consulate work at Trinidad, reminding Eberhardt and the State Department that he spoke French and not Spanish. Cipriani credited his social graces with helping him win the respect and friendship of the businessmen of Trinidad. He boasted of the work that he had done reporting on health issues and protecting the interests of American citizens in the country.

He complained that his salary at La Guaira was not enough to live on. He complained that the lack of money would require his son to leave college in the United States, and he complained that there was no school at La Guaira for his eleven-year-old daughter.

"Like a bolt from the blue," he wrote, "came a cable from the secretary of state advising the consul at Trinidad of the appointment of Mr. [John V.] Swearingen to my position, and so dropping me from the service. This was my recompense, after all, and hard as it seemed, almost unbelievable, I had to face the realization that hard work, a good clean record, efficient service, American citizenship, sometimes weighed naught in the scale of the department. Without the shortest notice, or slightest consideration, I had been thrown out of the service as might have been the veriest thief."

After a bitter recital of the various financial hardships that he had suffered, he wrote, "I had not been here more than a day when the consul informed me that it was quite impossible to support my family on the salary provided by the department, and with this cheerless news I returned to my family that evening. Had I but known the conditions that awaited my family here, I most assuredly would have resigned the service rather than accept the transfer to La Guaira."

Cipriani's letter-writing campaign continued into the spring. Again, he drew the attention of officials at Consular Services. Its director asked, "Is this another row?"

Clark was aware of Cipriani's unhappiness, and he learned of Voetter's upcoming reassignment to Antofagasta, Chile. He drafted two letters in April 1915. He wrote one to Voetter and one to Eberhardt. His bitter letter to Voetter scolded the consul for firing him.

> I am an older man than you, and I have had a wider experience of the world and of men than possibly the somewhat limited opportunities of a provincial life have afforded you. As a result of that experience, let me say to you that frankness, honesty, and sincerity in dealing with one's fellows always pays. That double-dealing, insincerity, underhand work, and injustice will surely recoil upon the man who adopts them!
>
> Your course toward me will have done you infinitely more harm than it could to me. Your own conscience will many times reproach you for what you have done. I do not doubt that it has already done so. No man of any intelligence

can be guilty of mean actions without having to regret it; and long after I shall have forgotten you, and what you have done or tried to do, you will remember it with self-reproach and regret.

Clark then said that in spite of it all, he bore Voetter "no ill will." He also revealed to Voetter that Eberhardt had questioned him about Voetter's competence during the post inspection.

He ended his letter by saying that he harbored "only my wishes for your welfare and success."

Cipriani was finally transferred, to Port Antonio, Jamaica, not Trinidad, in early 1916. Clark again marshaled his friends for a campaign to be reinstated at La Guaira. Writing from the Havlin Hotel in Cincinnati, Ohio, Dolge called on the director of Consular Services to see to it that Clark was reappointed. Dolge said, "A more loyal American, a more competent faithful officer it will not be possible to find. Mr. Clark's long residence in Venezuela, his knowledge of language and people, and his recognized high standing and friendly relations with the business community and Venezuelan government officials in all departments preeminently fit him for that office."

Carr inquired about what was happening with Clark's appointment. His assistant, H. C. Hengstler, replied that no action had been taken. He said that the matter was awaiting a report from the new consul.

Carr reminded Hengstler that Eberhardt had looked into the problems between Voetter and Clark. Eberhardt had concluded that the difficulty concerning Mr. Clark had "been largely due to personal feelings between the two men."

Meanwhile, the new consul, Homer Brett, responded to the department seventeen days after he was asked about the position. He was seeking more time to judge Clark.

He said that Clark had not yet applied for the position. He added, "I believe that if he should be appointed upon an application made direct to the department and not sent through the consul or endorsed by him, a most highly undesirable situation would be created."

If Clark applied, Brett wrote, it was his intention to offer him a temporary nomination as clerk. He urged the department to hold off on appointing someone to the vice consulship until he could "with further knowledge, advise more intelligently."

Brett already had formed an opinion of Clark, and it mirrored Voetter's opinion. However, he wanted Consular Services to believe that his rejection of Clark came only after his analysis of the man. He had discussed Clark with Voetter, and he was now wary of Clark. The next week, the consul was dead set against bringing Clark back to the consulate. He wrote a critical letter to the Office of the Secretary of State on March 25.

In one week, he would have Washington believe, he had learned much about Mr. Clark.

In consideration of his familiarity with the Spanish language, his reputation for industry, and his friendship with certain prominent members of the American colony, I had expected to advise his reappointment in spite of several valid objections to him, and I was surprised that when he knew of Mr. Cipriani's transfer he did not approach me in regard to the post.

Upon receipt of the department's instruction, I called upon the American minister, who has been

Mr. Clark's friend and much interested in having him reinstated, and I asked if he would suggest to Mr. Clark that he speak to me about the matter. The next day, the minister informed me that he had done so, but to his astonishment, Mr. Clark resented, or rather derided, the suggestion, and said, in effect, that his friends were quite capable of obtaining the appointment for him and that he neither needed nor desired any endorsement from the consul.

Later in his letter, Brett complained of a "whispering conspiracy" at the consulate that had targeted Voetter. He said that the conspiracy was "even against" him. Already, Clark's behavior had created a sense of antagonism between Brett and Clark.

One of the causes leading up to Mr. Clark's separation from the service was his habit of making derogatory remarks about Mr. Voetter and attempting to bring him into ridicule and contempt, and it appears that he now contemplates beginning a new term of service in a spirit of hostility and disdain toward another principal officer. In my case, there can be no possible personal reason.

Though I had, with misgivings, determined to overlook the objections to Mr. Clark, I think it well to state them here.

No one seems to know anything as to his history in the United States or the reasons for his protracted residence in Venezuela. His only home address on file here is that of a lawyer in New York City.

I recently took the registration books to Caracas and requested all individuals thought to be

American citizens to appear and register. Sixteen persons did so, and the only one invited who refused was Mr. Clark.

He is a man of false pretenses. He has at times given himself out as representing a group of Eastern capitalists seeking the concession for dredging Maracaibo harbor, but in view of his well known impecuniousness, it is improbable that he represents any capitalists whatever. I have heard that he strives to produce the impression that he is some sort of secret agent of the United States government, and I am convinced that to Venezuelans and some traveling Americans, he has represented himself to be American consul.

Through it all, Voetter remained steadfast in his opposition to Clark. Like Brett, he raised suspicions about him.

Toward the end of his evaluation report on Voetter, Eberhardt took note of Voetter's suspicions. In reference to Clark, Eberhardt quoted Voetter as saying, "There is something queer about a man of his age staying down in these countries as he does, remaining away from his family, caring to work for so small a salary as we pay. I don't know what it is, but there is something funny about him."

It had been eight years since the crime in New York. So far, the chameleon had managed to convince people that his new identity was legitimate. He had fooled everyone but Voetter and Brett. Neither man was prominent enough among his associates and superiors to be taken seriously.

Clark's handling of the new job opportunity at the consulate was dreadful. His arrogance was at its worst. The escapes and subsequent investigation by the Venezuelan government had preoccupied him and affected his judgment. His prospects for another job in Caracas or La Guaira were slim.

10

THE GATHERING STORM

C lark watched the events unfolding in Europe with dismay. He feared that the world war would draw in the United States, and he worried about what that would hold for him and for Venezuela.

His personal life was already in shambles. He had spent eight years as a fugitive. He had received no concession project from Gómez. He hadn't been home since 1909, and he hadn't seen his family since he fled New York in 1908. On the other hand, he'd stayed out of prison. He had avoided the humiliation of an arrest and trial, and there had been no sign that the police in New York harbored any interest in him.

In 1914, Voetter had ousted him from the legation. Brett had rejected his reinstatement in 1916. This left him with only a small amount of income from an occasional part-time job, and he was borrowing money again from friends in the United States. He accepted the loans without knowing how long they would last. The Red D steamship line brought mail in from the United States, and Clark's friends in New York smuggled funds in on its steamships. There was already talk that this line might suspend service because of German U-boat activities.

When he thought about his family and the likelihood of the United States joining the war, which he viewed as certain, he was nearly overwhelmed. He knew that the children would be fearful without their father's reassurance. He took comfort only in the knowledge that Anna and the children were living in the United States again.

He'd been renting a room from the Dolges at Plaza Panteón in Caracas. It was the lone positive aspect of his life, but that too was turning negative. The Dolges were generous. Boarding with them was as cheap as anything else Clark could find, and he enjoyed Mrs. Dolge's cooking, which came at no extra cost. The Dolges were occasional travelers with Dolge traveling more frequently than his wife. Clark's presence kept the house occupied. He looked after it when they were away, and they enjoyed his company when they were in Caracas.

During the first year of Europe's war, the US colony in Venezuela—like the United States—was split over which side it favored. That began to change with the sinking of the *Lusitania* in May 1915.

The sinking tested the relationship between the ministers in Caracas for a while. But by the spring of 1916, relationships had relaxed between the US and German ministers. McGoodwin went out of his way to arrange delivery of a check meant for German prisoners of war. The German community in Caracas had raised the money to buy clothes and cigars for the prisoners, who were interned on nearby Trinidad Island. McGoodwin was acting on the personal request of Herr A. von Prollius, the German minister in Caracas.

Shortly afterward, he passed along a report to Prollius from the US consul at Port of Spain who had delivered the clothes and cigars to the camp. It noted one hundred and seven

German POWs were interned there. It described how they were distributed in the camp. One soldier was confined to the insane asylum.

Five months later, McGoodwin was still unaware how much American opinion had turned against Germany. He inquired at the State Department about whether the United States could assure that Prollius would have safe passage to the United States if he traveled on a US ship. The German minister was worried that an English war vessel might encounter a US vessel, board it, and take him prisoner.

The State Department's reply was a decidedly huffy no. The effort showed, however, that the ministers remained outwardly on friendly terms.

Since that time, McGoodwin's public standing on the war remained inexplicably neutral. He was at odds with the majority of people in the US community in Venezuela. While not advocating the entry of the United States into the war, the people were turning decidedly against the Germans. Instead, McGoodwin's communications with the State Department were always focused on the war policies of Gómez and his government. He painted them as vehemently supportive of the Germans.

German designs on South America dated back centuries. Trade routes allowed for exchanges of coffee, tobacco, and cotton from Venezuela. Germans brought iron products, glass, and linens. In the years immediately preceding the outbreak of World War I, Venezuelan trade with Germany reached levels comparable to German trade levels with Peru, Cuba, and Colombia. German merchants dominated trade in Venezuela. From railways to coffee plantations, numerous German businesses were well established. Many of them had branches throughout the country.

Seeking to widen its sphere of influence, Germany viewed the less developed countries of South America as ripe for further colonization.

Germany viewed the United States as an enemy, and it saw the Monroe Doctrine and the control that the United States had of the Panama Canal as a threat to its own expansionist plans. Dating back to 1823, the doctrine proclaimed an end to further European colonization in the Americas and European interference in the sovereign affairs of the North and South American countries.

The battle for Venezuela's loyalty included establishment of German merchants in Venezuela. The German legation in Caracas courted the dictator and the leaders around him. German military officials found themselves welcome when they visited to take soundings of water depths along Venezuelan coastlines.

German war aims included naval bases and coaling stations in the Caribbean with open access to the Atlantic Ocean for its U-boats. Foreseeing that the United States would eventually enter the war, Germany also hoped to station U-boats close enough to harass shipping at the eastern end of the canal.

As the threat of war grew closer, Clark was astonished when he received a letter from the United States. It had been opened and sloppily resealed. On close examination, he noticed that other letters had also been resealed. He could make out double glue lines at the throats of the envelopes.

Gómez's operatives were known for censoring the mail. He first assumed that they were the culprits. He visited Red D Line captains at La Guaira to inquire about whether they were aware of any censorship of the mail that they carried in. They claimed not to be aware.

During calls at the legation, Clark was sometimes left alone for several minutes. He would covertly sort through the mail, but he couldn't convince himself that the sealed envelopes that he had found there had been tampered with.

He asked friends if they'd noticed anything odd about their mail, but no one had. He worried that he was being singled out, and he now assumed that US censors were responsible.

While his family and associates were always careful to use the Clark name, he recalled occasional references in the correspondence that might have attracted the scrutiny of an alert censor during wartime. He suspected that his outgoing mail was being censored as well.

In fact, he once sought to ruffle censors when he sent out several letters that were bound for the United States. He left them unsealed and wrapped together with a note saying that he wanted to spare them the bother of unsealing them.

He worried that any suspicion of him could lead to an investigation that might expose his past. He also began to worry that his friendship with the Dolges was a serious threat to his freedom.

He was correct to be concerned.

Although Dolge was born in the United States, the US diplomatic community in Venezuela thought that he was strongly supportive of the Germans. The word was slowly developing at the State Department and among military intelligence.

Clark watched Dolge's public tantrums over US positions on the war grow more strident. He then decided that he had to do everything possible to prevent the US authorities from becoming suspicious of him. He considered finding another place to live.

When he discovered that Dolge's mail was also being opened, he knew that his friendship with Dolge was no longer practical.

Using the censorship to his advantage, Clark began corresponding with Dolge when Dolge traveled in the United States.

Knowing that US censors would read his letters, he turned Dolge into his pawn. In one letter that he wrote to Dolge before the United States joined the war, Clark said that Dolge supported Germany too much. Clark portrayed himself as an enthusiastic patriot. Dolge was traveling in the United States at the time.

Clark cautioned Dolge that he was becoming "Germanized."

Clark retained copies and labeled them "Letters to an Ally, with pro-German leanings."

The ally was revealed in the letters with references to Don Rudolfo that were not very subtle.

"I fear you are getting completely Germanized about the war from your Cincinnati associates. Why did you join in sending these telegrams, identifying your intelligent and fair-minded self with the hyphenated propaganda?"

Clark portrayed himself as highly critical of the kaiser, and he referred to "the wrongfulness, duplicity, and bad faith" of Germany.

He concluded the letter:

> Well, old friend, so much for the war! I am glad we are not in it, and I attribute that fact largely to the wisdom and patience of President Wilson. Every German-American should be grateful to him and thankful that Teddy is not "on the job."
>
> I wish I could say as much for Wilson's Mexican policy, but I can't. Still, I am backing him for reelection.
>
> With best wishes, sincerely yours,
> C. N. C.

In another letter, Clark was scathing in attacking "a catalogue of atrocities." He mentioned Germany's "introduction of poisoning gases," and "the horrid crime of the *Lusitania.*"

He concluded that letter in a vague expression of his concern that he might be considered supportive of Germany.

> Now don't, for God's sake, tell any of your friends that I am pro-German, or even that I am a lukewarm ally, because the expressions of this epistle indicate a calm, judicial frame of mind.
>
> I am teetotally, exclusively, unqualifiedly, and unalterably a neutral American, who prays night and morning and between meals that the kaiser may get his and get it good and plenty!

In a third letter, he referred to the Zimmermann proposal to Mexico. He said that this was "quite sufficient to warrant a declaration of war on our part."

> The war news is almost thrilling! I am amazed at the crass stupidity of German diplomacy.

He mentioned a letter that he'd received from Dolge. Dolge discriminated between the German government and its people, and Clark disagreed with this. "They," he wrote, referring to the German people, "must be licked, Don Rudolfo, good and plenty. Licked to a standstill."

He concluded that letter with another call for the United States to declare war.

Dolge had purchased a home in Cincinnati after taking a position as the chief of foreign sales with the Wurlitzer family music business, which was based there. He continued to live for most of the time in Caracas, but the home in Cincinnati provided him a place to stay when he stopped over to visit the Wurlitzers. If the United States were to be drawn into the war, he intended to send his wife and his son to Cincinnati.

What had begun in Venezuela with his statements of anger and frustration over the war grew into an ever-deepening morass of suspicion of Dolge.

Cincinnati had become a final destination for many German immigrants who were making a new home in the New World. The German influx started in the 1830s. By the early 1900s, more than half of the residents in the city were immigrants from Germany.

Its loudest and most strident German loyalists were Rudolf and Howard Wurlitzer. They were the sons of Franz Rudolf Wurlitzer, the family's patriarch. They took over the music company when their father died in 1914.

In 1916, Howard Wurlitzer led a campaign protesting America's selling of munitions to the Allies. A storm of angry anti-German messages rained down on Washington.

Howard and Rudolf Wurlitzer were so publicly obnoxious that by the spring of 1917 their business had begun to slump, leading the family to appeal to the district attorney in Cincinnati for advice.

Clark's worries over possible exposure continued to grate on him. Over time, he became increasingly convinced that he'd have to leave Dolge's home, but he hadn't found an alternative.

As he'd promised Dolge, he was still running Dolge's business in Caracas, a laundry, while Dolge was away.

When Dolge returned, he planned to inform him that he'd found another place to live. He hoped he could convince Dolge of some false reason for leaving the household.

11

WAR IS HELL

On Monday evening of April 2, 1917, the man who "kept us out of war" did an about-face and asked Congress to declare war against Germany. Before dawn the next morning, Mrs. Dolge tapped on the door of her boarder at No. 3 Plaza Panteón in Caracas to announce a visitor. She was still dressed in her bedclothes.

Clark rose and picked up a robe from the foot of his single bed. He wrapped it around himself and then went to his bedroom door, opening it several inches.

Mrs. Dolge announced quietly, "Mr. McGoodwin is here to see you."

Clark was momentarily perplexed. Mrs. Dolge had never disturbed his sleep. She had never disturbed him at all. The minister was calling before the sun was up. Could this mean war? Had troops landed in Venezuela? He hadn't been sleeping well. He had been expecting the worst at any moment.

Clark explained that he would be right out to join the minister and Rudolf, who was back in Caracas.

Mrs. Dolge responded that McGoodwin hadn't asked to see Rudolf. He had only asked to see Clark. Mrs. Dolge turned around and returned to her bedroom.

Clark greeted the minister in the living room. He noticed that McGoodwin was short of breath and red-faced from exertion. Clark couldn't get him to sit down. He remained standing as the minister drew close. Their faces were almost touching.

Clark thought that he understood McGoodwin to say between gasps that he'd been out for hours. He'd been circulating through the US colony, ordering all to a war footing. He had been passing out surveillance assignments of known German agents and merchants around Caracas.

President Woodrow Wilson had declared war. Overnight, McGoodwin's attitude had turned decidedly aggressive. It unnerved Clark, who was already spooked because of his censored mail. He sensed that his life was out of his control. He hadn't felt this way since those days when he was planning his escape from New York. He was frightened by the weight of the moment and all that it portended.

As the conversation continued, it became clear to Clark that McGoodwin expected him to spy on the Dolges.

To appease McGoodwin for the moment, he nodded his head in consent. He did not inform the minister that he'd already begun looking for another place to live.

He'd thought it through. The news of his alleged spying on the Dolges might reach the State Department, but his problem was with military censors. Besides, he could make his own contacts inside the State Department.

The minister cautioned him not to inform Dolge about his efforts to organize the US colony. He also told Clark to not tell Dolge that he was being watched. Instead, McGoodwin advised Clark to simply explain to Dolge that McGoodwin was out calling on the Americans to stay calm and reminding them that Venezuela was unlikely to see combat.

He said that Clark should simply tell Dolge that the minister had seen no reason to wake him.

Within days, Clark was summoned to the legation with the other members of the US colony. They conducted a nighttime meeting to share what they had discovered. The Dolges were excluded.

Clark appeared early. Before the others showed up, Clark conferred with the minister, hoping to gain his support for a proposal for Clark to serve as a minister of information for the new group. He argued that his relationships inside the Venezuelan government and his connections with the press outlets in the United States made him the perfect candidate for the job. He suggested that the minister should introduce him as such when the others arrived.

It was a great opportunity, Clark thought, to show that he was as loyal as anyone. He hoped that the others would infer that he and the minister had worked together in planning the group's activities. He hoped that McGoodwin would share Clark's activities and enthusiasm with everyone.

Clark reminded McGoodwin that within two days of Wilson's speech, he'd translated it into Spanish and he had compiled an appropriate mailing list. Clark explained that he was about to send a letter to the secretary of state, informing him of the printing and distribution of ten thousand pamphlets. These pamphlets conveyed the war message to all members of the Venezuelan congress, the US colony, General Gómez, and his staff. It also conveyed the message to the top leaders of all twenty Venezuelan states, the governor of the Federal District, all postmasters and customs officials, all prominent citizens, and all legations throughout the country.

His friend Phelps, he explained, had paid for it.

McGoodwin was delighted that Clark had involved Phelps. Everyone in the Latin America Division at the department knew his name. He opened the meeting with an announcement about Clark's appointment.

In his follow-up dispatch, McGoodwin informed the State Department that they had ostensibly held the gathering to play bridge. He was hoping to keep the activities of the group secret. Actually, the regular card game that the American legation was known for during McGoodwin's tenure wasn't bridge. It was poker. They played poker into the early hours of the morning. They played for money and they drank whiskey, which the minister ordered twenty cases at a time. Certainly, no one would take notice of another late-night poker game among the Americans, war or no war.

Among their findings, the group discovered the recent installation of a windmill on some property that a German owned. The windmill was suspected to be a ruse for hiding a radio transmitter. A further search of the property concluded that it was a suitable fueling station for German U-boats. Germans residing near the coastline were drawing the most scrutiny.

McGoodwin was rewarded with a response from Secretary of State Robert Lansing, who praised the organizational efforts and said that he had read the report "with great interest."

Pleased with Lansing's response, McGoodwin suggested to the department that his plan of organizing the US community was worthy of being emulated throughout other South American countries and possibly beyond.

Now that the United States was in it for real, the tug-of-war for Gómez's sympathy began in earnest. The United States pressured Gómez to declare war against Germany. Short of that, they at least wanted him to maintain strict neutrality and condemn Germany's U-boat policies on the high seas. Gómez, however, remained aloof.

McGoodwin was charged with swaying Gómez to the side of the United States.

His efforts started badly. McGoodwin was dissatisfied after he saw the contents of the annual presidential address that Venezuela's provisional president, Victorino Márquez Bustillos, was going to deliver. So, he organized a diplomatic boycott of the address, enlisting the ministers of Britain, France, Italy, Cuba, and Belgium, to also stay away.

Most of the message dealt with a routine eulogy to Gómez. Bustillos didn't align Venezuela with the United States. He didn't forever rule out a break with Germany, but he said that if a German submarine attack were to kill Venezuelans or cause a loss of property to Venezuela, he would reconsider such a break. Gómez hadn't shifted far.

Then came revelations in the international press that Venezuela was selling the island of Margarita, which was just off its coast, to Germany. Germany, it was reported, intended to buy the island to locate a U-boat fueling base.

The reports drastically complicated McGoodwin's efforts. On May 24, he telegraphed a short dispatch to the department to say that the Venezuelan government was considering the sale and that "German propagandists have convinced Venezuelan authorities that submarine boats will be in the Caribbean soon after June 1, 1917," which was only days away.

The prospect of Margarita being in German hands upset the residents there. A number of them traveled to Caracas. Under the cover of darkness, they crept one by one into the US consulate, avoiding the secret police that Gómez had posted there. The residents unanimously favored the selling of their island to the United States.

In Washington, the president too was alarmed.

On June 1, President Wilson responded to the documents and dispatches about Margarita that Lansing had sent to McGoodwin. He assured Lansing that they had his attention, and he acknowledged the secretary's instructions to McGoodwin.

"As you suppose, I had already seen these telegrams and had read them with deep concern," Wilson wrote. "The dispatch you have sent is admirable, and I hope that you will follow the matter up in such a way that they will realize down there that any failure to comply with our representations and to give us assurances that can be relied on will be construed as amounting to hostility toward the United States."

The United States meant to leave no doubt about the severity of the Margarita issue.

Lansing's lengthy instructions to the minister carried a severe message that was all sticks and no carrots. It carried the threat that if Gómez didn't change course, the gates of hell would be thrown open. Torrents of angry exiles in the United States were sworn to overthrow him, and they were restrained only by the good graces of the United States.

Lansing marked his dispatch to McGoodwin, "URGENT."

> You will immediately demand an interview with General Gómez and say to him in substance the following:

> From various sources reports have reached this government that the government of Venezuela is contemplating the sale or lease of the Island of

Margarita to the German government or its agents or to German subjects. This government is loath to believe the truth of these reports, but their persistence and repetition from independent and heretofore reliable informants make it the duty of this government to lay the matter before General Gómez.

This government, while unable to ignore the information in its possession, conceives that General Gómez himself must be ignorant of the proposed action which is hostile to the spirit of Pan Americanism and to the Monroe Doctrine, which was twenty years ago invoked successfully for the benefit of Venezuela.

It, therefore, hopes and expects General Gómez to make an immediate and thorough investigation and to relieve this government of all apprehension by full assurances that such steps as have been taken looking to the transfer of Margarita will be cancelled and that no further action will be permitted in view of the fact that to permit action would be in direct violation of neutrality, which the government of the United States would be forced to consider as a breach of the traditional friendship which has existed between the two countries.

You may add that, in view of the reliable character of the reports and their serious nature, this government has felt compelled to lay the matter before the government of Brazil and other governments which have severed diplomatic relations with the German government, but advising them to withhold judgment and delay action until General Gómez has had an opportunity to consider the matter, as, however convincing the proof may seem and however necessary immediate action may appear, this government would prefer to suffer the consequences of delay rather than to do an injustice to the government of Venezuela by assuming that it would commit an act of unfriendliness to the American republics which have been forced by the German government to declare a state of war to exist between themselves and that government.

You may, provided it seems opportune, refer General Gómez very discreetly to the vigilance this government has constantly shown to interrupting and preventing expeditions or revolutionary movements against the government of Venezuela from being organized in or leaving the United States, and to impress upon him that a reciprocal spirit of friendship ought to impel him to prevent the use of Venezuelan territory directly or indirectly by the enemies of the United States and to suppress all intrigues and plots against the national safety of this country.

General Gómez cannot expect this government to continue its present policy of restraining his enemies if he does not pursue vigorously the same policy toward the foes of the United States. Both justice and friendship require reciprocal action.

It was a dangerous mission to assign to McGoodwin.

Before the minister could arrange a meeting with Gómez, an enemy surfaced within his own organization. His new minister of information was following another script, which was radically at odds with McGoodwin's accounts to the State Department.

While McGoodwin consistently argued that Gómez and the rest of the Venezuelan government were pro-German, Clark was more sympathetic in his newspaper articles, portraying Gómez and his policies as neutral. There were, after all, bills to pay. With the United States now in the war, Clark was being paid well.

The first cable that Clark sent to the Associated Press regarding the provisional president's address had irked McGoodwin. Clark made no mention of the boycott of the address that was arranged by the US minister. Further, in his cable, Clark contradicted McGoodwin. Clark described Venezuela's neutrality as credible and legitimate.

Clark started working on the Margarita issue as soon as it arose, approaching Andrade for an interview. The minister was happy to comply.

On June 16, Clark cabled the Associated Press to say that General Andrade had unequivocally denied that "Germany or [its] interests have sought purchase Island Margarita or any concession there or elsewhere." Andrade was the former president, and now he was Clark's personal emissary inside the Venezuelan government. Clark said that Andrade attributed the reports to "enemies of present government." On July 1, the story appeared in the *New York World* under the headline: "No Inch of Venezuela Can Germany Obtain."

The story attributed the denial to Andrade. It concluded, "Sensational reports of revolutionary uprisings in Venezuela published earlier in certain New York newspapers are untrue. The Gómez government enjoys absolute order in all parts of the republic."

McGoodwin called on Clark to account for this cable. Clark learned that McGoodwin was questioning his loyalty at the State Department. Clark responded quickly. He distributed another article in August to refute what he told the secretary of state were "scurrilous insinuations of German propaganda, attributing sinister designs on the part of the United States toward the countries of Spanish America."

The breach between Clark and McGoodwin widened quickly. By September, McGoodwin was railing to the department about Clark, reporting that Clark was accepting money from General Andrade for writing articles in support of Gómez and referring to Venezuelan war neutrality as absolute.

At the same time that he was accepting funds from Andrade, Clark was accepting payments for articles that he was sending to the Associated Press. His own writings and comments to others later confirmed this.

McGoodwin's dispatches to the State Department also confirmed this. It was clear that the close friendship between the minister and his former vice and deputy consul had crumbled. In one of his dispatches, McGoodwin said the following to the State Department:

> One American citizen here, whose regard for General Gómez and perquisites outweigh his sense of decency and duty, was sending news articles and editorial page communications to New York newspapers, attempting to show Gómez is a genuine friend of the United States.

As acting correspondent of the Associated Press, the only American or Ally news association which has ever been able to secure service from Venezuela, on account of the invariably and unreasonably strict censorship, the individual referred to above reported that the cabinet named by General Gómez on September 7 was "pro-Ally."

He came to me with a sickly grin three days later and declared that the censor would not allow him to report otherwise and then, even so, his cablegram to Associated Press had been held up three days to be read to General Gómez personally. He admitted that he had been taking eighty dollars from General Andrade, minister for Foreign Affairs, for each article he wrote that was favorable to the Gómez government.

It is true that this person is in very straightened circumstances, but I took the liberty of stating to him that the American colony would prefer to render assistance rather than have him misrepresent the local situation to the only international news association which maintains a correspondent in Caracas.

Weeks later, McGoodwin again skewered Clark, criticizing him for biased reporting in the American press. This time, McGoodwin called Clark "one careless American." Again, McGoodwin stated that the writer was working under the commission of General Andrade, and he was paid well "to answer or refute editorial references in three New York City newspapers."

Clark's self-serving interests became apparent in a letter that he wrote to the chief of the Associated Press, in which he continued to support Gómez and called the claims that the government was pro-German a fabrication. Clark reminded Melvin Stone, the chief of the Associated Press, about Clark's stories sent to AP over the last year, including the Venezuelan government's denial that it had been considering selling Margarita to Germany.

> In addition to my own ability to judge the truth of conditions in Venezuela, I have taken up the subject with General Ignacio Andrade, the minister of the Interior [chief minister] here and a thorough-going pro-American as well as ex-president of Venezuela, and he has authorized me to give unqualified denial to every assertion and implication that Venezuela or the Venezuelan government has been, even in the slightest degree, other than strictly neutral, or that it has either directly or indirectly favored or aided Germany.

12

WHEN THE SPIES CAME

W hile Venezuela did not become a field of combat, it wasn't spared the cloaks and daggers that the war in Europe had dispersed around the globe.

Assigned to oversee US military intelligence in the country was Capt. Robert Kemp Wright.

His stiff bearing and his stern, disapproving countenance announced him as an indisputable figure of authority.

Wright knew his way around the country. He'd been there before. In 1904, he'd been sent down as the manager of the New York & Bermudez Company, a US firm that had become ensnarled in a lawsuit for its financing role in the Matos Revolution against Cipriano Castro in 1901 and 1902. Wright's wife and son were with him then. This time he came alone.

He arrived at Puerto Cabello, where the Venezuelan Naval Yard was located. Shortly afterward, Wright began informing US residents that he was a secret agent of the United States Navy. When he got around to calling on the American legation at Caracas, he informed McGoodwin that he was in Venezuela to look into copper-mining concessions. He hadn't bothered to call on the minister until he'd been in the country for six months.

Wright's deceptions, along with McGoodwin's widely recognized paranoia about new American arrivals in the country, made him persona non grata at the legation. The enmity between Wright and McGoodwin began when McGoodwin tried to order Wright to follow a suspected German agent to Curacao. Their dispute was initially personal, but it grew into an all-out battle that split America's resident diplomatic and military communities.

Not by accident, Clark came to associate with the captain, whom he referred to as "the Commodore." Clark described the captain as a "fine fellow and pleasant companion, an American sleuth with a tremendous suspicion complex."

According to Clark, Wright's "sleuth aspect" was so unmistakable that "anybody could divine what he was up to."

Wright, he wrote, viewed all Germans, and especially certain German-Americans, "with great distrust almost amounting to hostility."

Rudolf Dolge was on Wright's suspect list, even before the captain arrived. They knew each other from Wright's first assignment in Venezuela. At the time, Dolge represented the Orinoco Company, which was also being sued for supplying money to the Matos Revolution. The two men had been in contact regularly. Their common business for different companies led them to distrust each other. The second time around, their different positions on the war worsened their relationship significantly.

Clark began to see the perfect roommate in Wright. He saw someone who might be willing to divert the attention of the US military intelligence operatives. Surely, no one would suspect a roommate of the captain to be an agent of Germany.

As soon as word got out that Wright was in the country to oversee military intelligence, Dolge informed Clark about his differences with Wright. Clark responded immediately, approaching

Wright to raise his suspicions about Dolge's loyalties. Clark quoted Dolge's tirades against the position of the United States in the war.

Clark also set out to influence Wright against McGoodwin, hoping Wright's credibility at the State Department could injure McGoodwin's credibility and reputation there.

Wright spent his first months traveling throughout the US colonies at Puerto Cabello and Caracas. He recruited Americans who were competent and willing to help him track the activities of the Germans.

Another player was new to Venezuela, and his arrival created a stir in the colonies of the United States and Germany.

In early September 1917, McGoodwin informed the State Department that a highly suspicious man holding an American passport and claiming to represent the Associated Press had called at the legation, giving the name of John Peter Jens Duhn.

McGoodwin said that Duhn had presented himself to others and he carried a card saying that he was a representative of Staats-Zeitung, a publication circulated among Germans who were living in New York. Duhn, he said, spent his first two days in Caracas visiting more than a dozen of the most active German propagandists who were in residence there.

Duhn said that he would be traveling to the interior of the country before going to Colombia. McGoodwin instructed the American consul in Puerto Cabello to interview the officers of the *Philadelphia,* the steamship that Duhn had arrived on, and then report back.

The consul, Frank Anderson Henry, responded quickly, saying that Duhn had represented himself on the ship as a newspaperman. He said that Duhn spoke with a foreign accent, and he was twenty-three or twenty-four years old.

One week later, McGoodwin complained to the department that Duhn had told the US consul at La Guaira that he was in the secret service of the United States Navy, but he had not mentioned this when he had talked to McGoodwin. McGoodwin again brought up his problem with Wright, who by then had still not informed the minister that he was a US intelligence officer. McGoodwin also complained that Wright had recently visited Maracaibo to speak with a third naval intelligence agent named A. G. Lamas. Lamas would pick up his mail at the legation when he was in Caracas, but he had never mentioned to the legation staff that he was working for naval intelligence.

"These three are still in Caracas," McGoodwin said. "Their services could be used by this legation if they are employees of the government of the United States. Please advise by telegraph also as to Addison H. McKay of Washington who has left the impression with Venezuelans, including Venezuelan officials, that he is a confidential agent of the United States. He came here three weeks ago."

McGoodwin grew resentful about being kept in the dark, and he was unhappy that he seemed to no longer be in charge of the US war strategy in Venezuela. Two days later, he sent a terse cable to the department, reporting that Wright had informed the consul at La Guaira that a fourth secret service operative was due to arrive in the country immediately to operate on the Orinoco River.

In its first response, the State Department only asked McGoodwin to inform it about the whereabouts of Duhn.

A second cable, which was marked secret and confidential, came back in the middle of September from the secretary of state. It made clear that Wright was "hands off."

R. K. Wright, A. G. Lamas, and J. Duhn are engaged in confidential work for the Office Naval Intelligence.

Wright, enrolled as lieutenant in reserve force, is in charge of the work in Venezuela. Other two are under him.

On account of special work in which Wright is engaged, it is not deemed advisable that he work at legation. Should you have any investigation work to be done, Office of Naval Intelligence is glad to give Wright instructions in this regard.

McKay is unknown. Greatest discretion must be observed in communicating with Wright.

The rebuke over McGoodwin's contact with Wright had come quickly. Wright complained to his military supervisors about an "indiscrete contact" that McGoodwin had made, and the military supervisors forwarded his complaint to the State Department.

McGoodwin felt like he had to defend himself, and he feigned innocence when he explained his contact to the department. It wasn't a convincing account.

He said that he had telegraphed Wright at Puerto Cabello on August 7 as an American citizen "whose services were needed at that particular time." He needed to get passage on a steamship that was bound for Curacao so that he could follow a German naval reserve officer who was aboard.

At his disingenuous worst, McGoodwin said that he couldn't have possibly known that Wright was an intelligence operative at the time, as Wright had never informed the legation. McGoodwin lied, stating that he had first learned of this from a recent cable that Lansing had sent him, in which Lansing had responded to McGoodwin's inquiry about Wright, Duhn, and Lamas.

"I did not communicate with Captain Wright officially; he had not informed the legation of his connection with the government of the United States. Had he done so during the many opportunities that had been presented, since his arrival [in Venezuela] on February 22nd last, the legation would have acted accordingly. Had Captain Wright given even an intimation of his real purpose here, instead of representing that he came to acquire concessions for copper mines, he would have been supplied very, very discreetly with information which he should have had."

Two weeks later, Wright got even. Navy intelligence had made a blistering assessment of McGoodwin, and this assessment had arrived at the State Department's Office of the Counselor. Assistant director of ONI, Henry Knox, said that "a reliable source in Venezuela" had told him that McGoodwin wasn't up to the job of minister. Knox was clearly referring to Wright.

The report said that McGoodwin's "lack of tact and continual blundering" had left most American and Venezuelan officials against him.

"The chief of the German Secret Service here thinks our minister is one of his best assistants and does not hesitate to say so to those whom he thinks he can trust."

The dispatch concluded, "American minister under suspicion. The German legation knows all that takes place in our legation."

Facing off against Wright's agents was a highly trained group of German agents who began arriving in the country two months before the United States entered the war.

The Germans operated in a climate that was mostly favorable to them. The German merchants already had been organizing in Venezuela. The dictator adopted German military dress and mannerisms, and he jailed editors who printed material that was negative about him or his policies toward the war. Venezuela pledged to maintain "strict neutrality" toward the war, but US leaders viewed this claim with skepticism.

The leader of the German spy ring in Venezuela was the notorious Captain Erich Hirschfeld. He was a man with a storied past.

Hirschfeld first came to the attention of US military intelligence when he was released from internment in 1914 from a British prisoner camp.

Hirschfeld had moved to the United States in 1908, living on 76th Street in Brooklyn. In 1913, he was working as a fourth officer on a US ship, the *Kroonland* of the Red Star Line, when it came to the aid of the American liner *Volturno,* on October 9 as it burned at sea.

More than one hundred people perished in the accident. Hirschfeld's role in saving the crewmen of the *Volturno* earned him a medal from the US Congress, and he carried a letter from the US commerce secretary that acknowledged his heroics and the medal. His actions in the rescue were cited in 1914 in an application for his release from the British war camp.

He'd laid low in Maracaibo after arriving in Venezuela. He preceded the other agents, arriving in February of 1917.

In the middle of June, he took a steamship to Caracas and immediately called on the American minister. He brought a declaration of intention that had been issued by a court in Brooklyn. It declared that he wanted to become an American citizen.

McGoodwin refused to register him. Hirschfeld attempted to overcome McGoodwin's objections, explaining that he'd purchased three warships and hoped to purchase more. He explained that this would require traveling. The Red D Line, he told the minister, had refused him passage to Caracas because he was German. Hirschfeld also produced papers showing that he'd served as an officer aboard US civilian vessels, and he showed the minister his letter from the secretary of the Department of Commerce.

Delighted by Hirschfeld's arrival, the German legation at Caracas boasted to the German colony that Hirschfeld was responsible for supplying Berlin with "proof in advance" that the *Lusitania* was armed and carrying ammunition. A German U-boat had sunk the ship after the Germans had received this information. The rumor quickly found its way to the US colony and the US minister, who passed it along to the secretary of state.

Hirschfeld was no lightweight in the world of espionage. Before arriving in South America, he was known to US military intelligence as a member of the German Imperial Navy. He was an expert at laying mines. He'd worked in New York with the even more notorious Captain Karl Boy-ed, the naval attaché to the German minister to the United States, Franz von Papen.

Hirschfeld worked on neutral vessels that were bound for Europe, part of the German attempt to obstruct US aid to the war efforts of the Allies, ever vigilant for any ship carrying armament or ammunition for Germany's enemies.

Hirschfeld had already gained favor with Gómez. He advertised himself as a naval engineer in Venezuela to give Gómez a "plausible reason" for hiring him as superintendent of the Venezuelan Navy Yard at Puerto Cabello. Hirschfeld also carried a Venezuelan license as a wireless operator. US operatives became aware that he was in charge of the German Secret Service in Venezuela and Colombia, and he had been appointed chief of Venezuela's secret service.

He was described in US military intelligence reports as "strongly built; weight one-hundred-seventy-five pounds; fair hair; clean shaven; and very insolent, pro-German manner."

13

MISSION ABORTED

The lights at the Barnacle burned late into the night as the resident Americans who were charged with combating German war efforts gathered for drinks, poker, and war talk.

Wright, Clark, and Addison McKay shared the Barnacle, a cottage in Caracas, and they hosted the nightly gatherings. Others from the US colony dropped in when they were summoned.

Doyle, who had left the State Department in 1913 to join the Caribbean Petroleum Company as its attorney in Caracas, attended most of the meetings. He wanted to keep an eye on McKay, whom he feared had come to Venezuela to exploit its petroleum reserves for US companies. He also needed to receive early knowledge of US war activities that might harm British petroleum interests in the country. CPC was a British-owned company, but Doyle wasn't about to concede the point.

German intentions in South America included drawing Gómez into the war on Germany's side, attaining a fueling base for German U-boats in Venezuela, expanding German influence throughout South America, and possibly harassing US and Allied ships on the eastern entrance of the Panama Canal.

A regular topic of conversation was the deplorable civilian representation of the United States in the country, namely the American minister. Clark would usually instigate these conversations. McGoodwin was never invited to these gatherings.

In these nightly meetings, Clark learned about Wright's mischievous plots to contest the Germans and to embarrass McGoodwin when possible. Clark and Wright were building a friendship, as Clark fed Wright's contempt for the minister.

He'd chosen, he thought, the safest place to live. Wright's reputation for supporting the US war effort was well known in military intelligence and State Department circles. Clark had become Wright's close associate. Clark's daily access to Wright also gave him opportunity to encourage Wright's deep distrust of McGoodwin and his good friend Charles Freeman, who visited the US legation on an almost daily basis. Wright believed that Freeman was a German loyalist who leaked information that he had gathered at the US legation to the German legation in Caracas. Clark believed that the worse McGoodwin looked to the State Department, the less weight his criticisms of Clark would carry.

Clark was enjoying the time of his life. By working alongside Wright, he fulfilled his insatiable need for intrigue, of which there was never a shortage.

With several years of training at wartime espionage, the German agents who had been sent to Venezuela in 1917 held a decided advantage against the fledging US operation. The only weakness on the part of the Germans was the dedicated mole who was in their midst.

Born in Hamburg, Germany, Duhn had grown unhappy with the rising militarism in Germany. In 1908, he had immigrated to the United States at the age of sixteen. He had left Germany after a group of German soldiers roughly bullied him off of a sidewalk in his hometown of Hamburg.

He was handsome and blue-eyed, and he was five-foot-seven. The fiery, uncompromising young operative was willing to take on the most dangerous risks, and he frequently planned and executed his own missions.

Time and again, he found ways to neutralize the Germans. Although he didn't become a naturalized citizen of the United States until 1919, he was readily accepted into service after walking into ONI offices in Washington and volunteering to serve as a double agent.

He spoke English with a German accent, and he was knowledgeable of all things German. The German agents in Venezuela immediately greeted him as one of their own. He spent many of his early days in Caracas calling on German businesses. These businesses were deftly evading the wartime trade restrictions that the United States had poorly implemented. He introduced himself to Hirschfeld, who immediately hired him as his chief assistant at the Venezuelan Navy Yard at Puerto Cabello. Within a month, he'd moved in with Hirschfeld.

Duhn had originally seen Hirschfeld's commission as a wireless operator from the Venezuelan government, and alerted Captain Wright that Hirschfeld held it. Duhn knew whatever Hirschfeld knew at the moment he knew it.

Within weeks of Hirschfeld hiring him, Duhn was leading several German agents and Venezuela's minister of war around the navy yard when he overheard an astonishing statement from the minister of war. Again, he passed on the information to Wright, who reluctantly passed it on to McGoodwin. It was too incredible to withhold.

McGoodwin informed Washington of what he called the "remarkable announcement."

"Incredible as it may seem, Gómez has decided that if he is to be dragged into the war, he will take sides with Germany. This decision was reached on Saturday, October 27th and was communicated to Hirschfeld and a group of influential Germans by Dr. [Carlos Jiménez] Rebolledo, Venezuelan minister of War and Marine at Puerto Cabello."

The announcement, he wrote, was made "in the presence of an operative of the United States intelligence office."

Gómez, he said, "actually believes there is danger of invasion by troops of the Allied governments, including the United States."

McGoodwin then explained the dangerous seeds that Hirschfeld had planted in the Gómez government.

> Diagrams of proposed mine fields and plans for blowing up the highways which connect Caracas with La Guaira and Valencia with Puerto Cabello were taken to Gen. Gómez at Maracay Wednesday. It was arranged for him to meet Herr A. von Prollius, the German minister, four influential German friends and advisers of General Gómez, Hirschfeld, and three Venezuelan naval and army officers, (two of them Germans) at San Juan de los Morros on Friday, November 2nd. The meeting took place as scheduled, Herr von Prollius having motored from the health resort of Los Teques and, from the best information obtainable, the plan as regarded the mines was decided upon.
>
> Hirschfeld was to have proceeded immediately to the Puerto Cabello Navy

Yard if Gómez approved his scheme;
otherwise, he had arranged to return to
Caracas. This much is certain. He went
directly to Puerto Cabello, accompanied by practically all of the conferees
except, of course, Gómez.

McGoodwin warned Washington about the large stocks of explosives that were at the navy yard, and he mentioned that a yacht
was available for transporting these explosives.

There is danger of dash in converted vessel, one
of which was a reasonably fast American yacht.

He'd discovered that the State Department regarded the
Panama Canal as having a high risk of being attacked, and he
mentioned that it was a possible target.

The imbroglio between the United States and Venezuela was
at a critical point when Duhn learned the real reason a schooner
was berthed at the navy yard.

Hirschfeld and his agents were up to something quite different than planning an attack on the Panama Canal. They
were covertly stealing equipment from German ships that
were interned around the Caribbean, and they were load-
ing this equipment aboard the vessel. Duhn revealed that the
Germans were on a mission to break out of the Caribbean
Sea. They planned to travel into the Atlantic and head directly
north. They were bound for Greenland or Iceland, and they
planned to then head east to Norway. Germany was the final
stop. In Germany, they would unload the machinery for the
war effort.

Duhn learned every detail. He'd be second in command to Hirschfeld on the mission.

After being informed, Captain Wright immediately arranged for a navy warship to be on standby at Curacao. Wright intended to travel to Curacao to direct an operation to intercept, board, and seize the schooner and arrest the men onboard.

As the three plotters huddled over the plan at the Barnacle, Wright was at his worst. He was fretting over whether to involve McGoodwin. In Wright's view, Hirschfeld was the most dangerous German agent in the country. McGoodwin, he felt, was the second.

At the least, Wright feared a leak and he had good reason. He regularly watched in astonishment as Hirschfeld visited the US legation at will. Wright also distrusted Freeman, the man who had first proposed the sale of Margarita to Germany as a navy base. Freeman was McGoodwin's best friend in Venezuela.

Some people alleged that Freeman had recently been known as the "enthusiastically pro-German Karl Lieberman."

Freeman had worked as the manager at American Mining and Magnesite Co. on Margarita. In 1916, he'd written to the German consul general in New York, informing him that he had "a place which was suitably prepared for a base." He offered it as such. US censors at Trinidad intercepted the letter, but they never forwarded it. Instead, they sent it back to Freeman with the note, "Freeman, do not be a fool."

Prior to the United States declaring war, Freeman was openly pro-German, and he decorated his car with German flags when news came of German victories in the war. Freeman was another regular at the US legation, and Wright believed that he was the one passing on everything that went on there to the Germans.

That was his most positive view. At worst, he feared direct sabotage by McGoodwin.

Duhn was still at the navy yard. Wright's plan called for Duhn to relay the time and date of the departure of the schooner, but no one had explored how that would be accomplished. With Duhn at Puerto Cabello and Wright at Curacao, only the US legations at Curacao and Caracas had the means to communicate the start of the mission quickly to the others involved.

Wright concluded he had no option but to use McGoodwin. He instructed Clark to spend as much time as possible at the legation house and try to keep Freeman away from the minister. Clark was hopeful that Wright would mention his direct role to the State Department and the Office of Naval Intelligence.

McGoodwin was excited by the prospect of striking a blow to the Germans, and he was excited about how this would make him look at the State Department. He enthusiastically signed on. The US consul at Curacao was the intermediary.

Wright left Venezuela for Curacao.

Captain Edward McCauley, the assistant director of the Office of Naval Intelligence, would have the task of explaining what went wrong to his naval superiors.

Duhn and some Germans from Colombia and Venezuela were taking some instruments from interned German ships and were all ready to sail from Puerto Cabello due E on the 11th or 12th parallel, to a point of Longitude that goes north and south on the Atlantic and then go north to Greenland or Iceland, then over to Norway.

Captain Wright had advised the department here of this contemplated trip, and left it to the minister to advise him when they started.

McGoodwin devised a telegraph code that he agreed to send to Wright at Curacao. Duhn was to secretly send a message to the American consul at Puerto Cabello as soon as he learned when the schooner would sail, and the consul was to alert McGoodwin.

Wright was quoted at length in McCauley's report.

The message was to inform the consul that a friend of Duhn's had arrived for a stay of four or five or six or however many weeks. Is it necessary to register at this consulate?

In the message, the number of weeks that was listed for the length of the friend's purported stay represented the date in October that the schooner would sail.

McGoodwin promised to forward the message to the American consul at Curacao, who would then inform Wright. The consul was then supposed to telegraph the return coded message to McGoodwin at Caracas.

McCauley quoted Wright:

When the party that intended to go on the schooner was about ready to leave, No. seventy-nine [Duhn's assigned ONI number] laid the whole matter before the minister, who promised to help in every way, and I left for Curacao in order to communicate with the ship [the US naval vessel] to inform them of any change of program.

The only way seventy-nine could communicate with me was through the American minister, unless we took someone else into our confidence, and the minister himself arranged the plan. I am enclosing the notes on the plan in the minister's own handwriting, and also a letter from him which was to remind me of the key words of the disguised cables.

The plan went well at first. Wright arrived at Curacao with no indication of any leak to the Germans. He grew more confident, even with McGoodwin now involved.

In the event that there was any gunfire during the boarding, the officers on the US warship at Curacao asked for photographs of Hirschfeld and Duhn. They wanted to assure that Duhn would be safe, and Wright preferred to have Hirschfeld captured alive. McGoodwin was assigned to obtain the photographs.

Wright should have known better.

McGoodwin had no photograph of Hirschfeld, and he had little time to find one. He asked a Venezuelan photographer he knew to obtain four photographs of Hirschfeld. The photographer innocently decided to obtain the photographs from the German consul at Puerto Cabello, and in the process he explained to the consul that McGoodwin had asked him to obtain them.

The alerted German consul shortly remarked to Duhn, "Hirschfeld will now have to be very careful as the American minister is watching him."

When the German minister was informed, he realized that the mission was compromised and he scuttled it.

McGoodwin further aggravated Wright by not contacting him at Curacao once the mission was called off.

Wright was quoted again:

> When however the delay and change of plans did come, and which I am forced to think he helped to bring about, he refused to send me any message, as you will see in the enclosed reports from seventy-nine, thus keeping me in utter darkness two weeks longer than was necessary.
>
> The minister is determined to prevent any of us from doing anything useful here.

Wright called for McGoodwin to be recalled or reassigned.

> It really seems useless for our office to keep men here as long as the present minister remains to block their efforts, and if the Department of State could be induced to call him home by cable for consultation, or promote him to some other sphere of activity, in short, get him out of here for a few months, such action I believe would result in the greatest good, and there would then be some chance of bringing Venezuela peaceably into line with the rest of Latin America, which will never be done so long as he remains here to irritate and nag at them.

Wright concluded his report with a diatribe:

> I am afraid that what I think of our minister here, if adequately expressed, would not pass the

censor. Really, the minister, Mr. McGoodwin, is worse than Herbert W. Bowen, who was formerly minister here and who was kicked out of the service by John Hay as a crazy scoundrel and as a traitor to his department. See letter of dismissal of Bowen from President Roosevelt to John Hay in the Bowen-Loomis scandal in 1906.

Bowen was a drug fiend and in a way was crazy and irresponsible, but McGoodwin has no such excuse. He is simply malicious, jealous of other departments of the government, and I believe he is absolutely unprincipled.

Because of Bowen's actions as arbiter in the New York & Bermudez case, Secretary of State Hay recalled him in 1905. As manager of NY&B in Venezuela at the time, Wright was familiar with Bowen's actions.

When McGoodwin realized his mistake, he tried to escape blame in Washington by fabricating a story about the Germans scuttling the voyage of the schooner at the moment it was due to begin on orders from Gómez.

McGoodwin reported to the State Department that the dictator "required the services of Hirschfeld, first to superintend the transfer of two additional war vessels into merchantmen, for use in [the dictator's] privately owned company, a monopoly upon coastwise and river freight and passenger transportation, and secondly to construct and lay contact mines in the harbors and other points along the coast."

While Wright's mission to seize the schooner foundered, Clark's mission to poison McGoodwin's standing with him was a complete success.

14

THE EDITOR

Sleeping only a few hours each night after late hours of war plotting at the Barnacle, Clark arose early each morning to work at his day job, drafting articles about the war for US and Venezuelan newspapers.

On one morning, he paid a visit to the newspaper offices of *El Fonógrafo* in Caracas. He carried an article that he'd just completed, and he wanted to have it published immediately.

Carlos López Bustamante received him. López was a well-known editor with pro-Allied sentiments and two newspapers to express them.

Weeks before, he'd begun publishing in Caracas. Prior to relocating to Caracas, he had published his family's *El Fonógrafo* newspaper in Maracaibo. López learned the business while working as his father's assistant in Maracaibo. When the father died after nineteen years as the editor, the son took over. The war was going on and Maracaibo was a center of German influence, so he left his brother in charge of that newspaper and went to Caracas to work in what he hoped would be a friendlier atmosphere.

Clark introduced himself to the editor. He spoke in the man's language, hoping it would raise the editor's estimation of him.

He explained that his story was intended to refute an article that had appeared in a pro-German newspaper in Venezuela on the reasons the United States had entered the war. He had also intended to proclaim Venezuela's sincere adherence to its purported policy of "strict neutrality." He claimed that the government of Venezuela was a good and reliable friend of the United States, and he thought that Gómez was a great and caring leader.

He held out the story to assure that López saw that it was written in Spanish.

He hoped López would pay him as General Andrade was paying him. General Andrade had first commissioned the piece. Later, he had invited Clark to the government's offices so that Andrade could review it.

Andrade wanted the piece to appear soon in the local Caracas press, and he made sure that Gómez was portrayed as an ally of the United States and a benevolent leader of Venezuela. He intended it for local and international consumption, hoping that Clark would have it circulated throughout the United States. After all, Mr. Clark was a known representative of the Associated Press in Caracas. Andrade hoped that such an article, which was written by an American, would go far to counter the growing enmity between the governments.

Clark informed López that he was visiting the newspaper "upon the suggestion of Mr. McGoodwin." It was a lie. Clark expected the minister's name would overcome any possible objection to the article.

Clark left the editor's offices intending to check the newspaper daily, as he assumed that the article would soon be published.

López turned to the story immediately. He didn't like what he was reading. With no apparent concern, he called McGoodwin and told him that he found it too "flattering" to Gómez. He refused to print it. McGoodwin expressed surprise by the call, and he told the editor that he was unaware of Clark's article.

López soon came to regret his decision to not print the story.

Clark learned of the rejection in a letter from López a few days later. He contacted General Andrade on a Friday to explain why it hadn't appeared.

General Andrade requested Clark come to his office. Later in the afternoon, Clark appeared. After they had exchanged pleasantries and sat down, Clark held out the letter of rejection for Andrade. When Andrade looked up from reading it, Clark explained López's objections further. He quoted the editor as stating that the story was too positive about Gómez.

Hopeful that he would still be paid, Clark added that other newspapers in the country were soon planning to run the article. Andrade only nodded and smiled, leaving Clark with the impression that the general was satisfied. The weekend was coming and he gave the matter no more thought.

On Monday morning, the telephone rang at the business offices of *El Fonógrafo*. It was July 23, 1917. The Venezuelan government was ordering López to suspend the publication of his newspaper.

López immediately consulted the district prefect, General Lorenzo Carvallo, whom he later labeled "one of the many rascals surrounding Gómez." At midday, he published a leaflet announcing the closing of his newspaper, explaining that the prefect had ordered *El Fonógrafo* "suppressed from this date."

During the afternoon, he ignored urgent summonses from the government. Suspecting he was about to lose his freedom, he did what he could to get his business affairs in order, as he sought help to avoid being arrested and to save his newspaper.

López believed that his survival and that of his newspaper lay solely with the Allied ministers. Distrusting McGoodwin, he called on the British minister, Henry Beaumont, who had previously been supportive of López, his brother, and the newspaper in Caracas. Beaumont had even helped with some of the start-up costs.

Beaumont spoke to him only a few minutes before declaring the situation a serious one and stating that he, Beaumont, needed to call the American minister. López listened as Beaumont made the call in his presence. He understood enough of the conversation to know that McGoodwin agreed to be at the British legation "in a moment."

Confident that Beaumont understood the gravity of his situation and that the matter was being aggressively addressed, López left the British legation to avoid meeting face to face with McGoodwin.

The editor returned to the newspaper offices and waited. When he received no word from the British minister for several hours, he sent his brother-in-law to see Beaumont. His brother-in-law returned with distressing news. He told López that Beaumont had received him "unkindly," saying this "happened to us for publishing the sort of articles we did, knowing the country in which we lived."

López was stunned. The routine of passing along similar articles in support of the Allied war effort to López for publication had begun with the British legation. The only difference was that López refused to publish this article because it was so positive toward the dictator. López was puzzled because Beaumont had been so supportive in the past.

López later described to an agent at the State Department his shock at Beaumont's refusal to help.

He concluded that the American minister had convinced Beaumont that this was "not a diplomatic matter." He also concluded that Clark and McGoodwin were acting against him in concert.

"This is what they call in my country stepping on a mango rind [*poner una concha de mango*]," he would later say.

Explaining the suppression of the newspaper to the State Department, McGoodwin used the same words that Beaumont had used with López's brother-in-law.

The *El Fonógrafo* affair began with Andrade and Clark, but it played out at senior levels of the State Department, the White House, and the US press.

Beaumont and the secretary of the British legation advised López "to go into concealment."

Instead, the thirty-one-year-old editor spent the night at his home in Caracas. As instructed, he reported at nine-thirty the next morning to the Government House. From there, he was taken to police court. The chief of police, Pedro García, issued a warrant to the governor of the La Rotunda prison.

López was allowed to contact no one. He was whisked through the bustling streets of Caracas in a closed carriage to La Rotunda. At ten o'clock, he was led into the prison's front lobby. The entire incarceration process took only thirty minutes. He would spend the next eight and a half months in leg irons at La Rotunda. At first, he was in the criminal ward. After a short time, he was sent to the political ward.

"Eight months I passed in sequestration, loaded with chains, enduring all kinds of suffering, and left to die like a dog, as I saw four companions die during these eight months. All for having trusted too much."

When he was released from La Rotunda in early May 1918, Carlos López was instructed not to try to leave the country.

He was specifically told not to go to the United States. He could, he was told, return to Maracaibo, his ancestral home and birthplace. He couldn't start up his newspapers again. His newspaper at Maracaibo had been shut down while he was imprisoned.

Purchasing a ticket on a US steamship that was bound for Maracaibo, the editor was stopped from boarding at La Guaira, and he went into hiding at the port. The government had retracted permission for him to travel to Maracaibo.

López reached out again to Beaumont, who had already advanced money to a second López brother, Enrique, to purchase passage to Madrid, Spain. He also addressed credentials to the British ambassador to Spain, and he sent them to Curacao for Enrique to pick up before sailing. Beaumont informed McGoodwin about what he had done, and he added that he had given Carlos three thousand bolivars since his release.

After spending twenty-four days in hiding, Carlos López Bustamante, wearing a disguise, escaped La Guaira with the help of the Colombian consul there. He made his way to Puerto Cabello, where it was less likely that he would be recognized. From there, he boarded the steamship *Philadelphia* and sailed for Curacao.

On June 6, 1918, he quietly boarded the steamship *Caracas* at Curacao. He traveled to Ellis Island, New York, where an excited American press awaited him. Using a false name, he carried a British passport, which Beaumont had given to him before he had left Venezuela.

On landing at Ellis Island, López electrified the US press with his allegations that there was a pro-German government in Venezuela, and he described the terrible conditions in its prisons.

When asked about German submarine bases at Margarita and along the coast of Venezuela, his responses were less than direct. In one instance, he answered, "I have documents with me which I will present to the United States government at Washington that show many intrigues against this country."

According to another account two days earlier, he "intimated" that German submarines were operating in Venezuelan coastal waters. He would later tell the State Department that he couldn't confirm the presence of German submarine bases in his country.

Certain embellishments in his comments to the press about his prison experience went beyond the description he later provided to the State Department. He was quoted in newspapers as saying that while he was in prison he was bound in such a way that he could not sit up or lie down. He also said that his cellmate had died of poisoning after eating food that was intended for López.

After the press's interest in him died down, López traveled to Washington, taking up residence at the Hotel Continental at Union Station Plaza.

The editor's goal was to convince the administration and the State Department that thousands of Venezuelans were being tortured and dying in its prisons. He wanted to convey that its dictator was pro-German and not friendly with the United States. He also wanted the United States to help remove Gómez from power, but he fell short of calling for armed intervention because he felt that this wouldn't be necessary. His view was that the dictator would be gone after one loud bark from its powerful neighbor to the north.

The editor left no doubt about his beliefs concerning the US minister. He was corrupt, and he was taking payments from Gómez in exchange for coloring the reports that he sent back to Washington. Actually, McGoodwin's reports at the time mirrored López's reports on the dictator's positions on the war.

Ten days later, López sent a second lengthy and detailed letter to President Wilson. In this typewritten letter, López described in pitiable terms his imprisonment and escape from Venezuela.

In a third letter, he begged Latin American Division Chief Jordan Herbert Stabler "to make all your best to the favor of my poor country, chiefly with regard to those political prisoners dying by inches in those horrible jails."

He offered to supply information about Venezuelan affairs and the wartime-trading blacklist. He enclosed a nine-page, single-spaced typed report entitled "How the Allies Are Represented in Caracas, Venezuela, S. A." It was marked confidential.

> Mr. Preston McGoodwin, American minister: Rumor has been current for some time in Caracas that the American minister is on exceedingly good terms with General Gómez, but with whom, however, he maintains no visible personal relations, and this has given rise to some observations I give below:
>
> Since 1915, about the end of August or beginning of September, an appropriation has been made of one million bolivars [twenty thousand dollars] charged to contingent expenses. This appropriation has been coincident with the annual trip of the American minister, it being noted at the same time that Mrs. McGoodwin in these three years has come on ahead of her husband.
>
> It is believed and said in Caracas that this million bolivars, whose destination has not yet been ascertained, is somewhat in connection with the

trip of the minister and that the advance journey of his wife is for the purpose of collecting a check, the minister not leaving for this country until after receiving a cable announcing payment or acceptance.

The fact is that whenever the international situation has appeared most serious for the Gómez government, and when all of us Venezuelans have felt more encouraged than ever for an international solution favorable to the liberty of our country, the arrival of Mr. McGoodwin has seemed to dispel every cloud on the horizon of Gómez.

Ellis Island records show that in 1915 the McGoodwins, Preston, Jean, and Preston Jr. traveled home together. In 1916, Preston traveled home alone. Possibly Jean and his son preceded him. In 1917, records show that Mrs. McGoodwin traveled home with her son, arriving in the United States in August. McGoodwin traveled home in December to defend charges against him unrelated to Gómez. The three returned to Caracas together in March 1918.

Focusing his rant on Clark, López wrote:

Mr. McGoodwin is on very friendly terms with the well-known Mr. Clark, an American citizen too. To know the moral caliber of this gentleman, it is only necessary to recall the book he published upon Gómez and his administration.

That some Venezuelans, unfortunate through circumstances more or less sad and unpardonable should resort to servile and shameful adulation for selfish interests is explicable, but that a foreigner should select such a method is really ugly and much more shameful still.

Unaware that McGoodwin and Clark were no longer close friends, López wrongly concluded that the two were working together with the Gómez government to shutter his newspaper and imprison him. In his view, McGoodwin and Clark sought to see an article positive about Gómez appear in *El Fonógrafo*. López felt that they were taking revenge because of his failure to publish this article.

McGoodwin sloughed it off in his first communication about the newspaper suppression to the State Department, saying that the facts of the closing of *El Fonógrafo* "were simply that the newspaper was abusive to the Venezuelan government and was suppressed for no other reason." However, he quickly found a better explanation. He hoped that this explanation would better serve his tenuous position in Washington.

Ten days after *El Fonógrafo* was shut down, an entirely new explanation was revealed. It was related to the department.

Gómez, McGoodwin said, had flown into a rage after being informed of the supposedly real US position toward Venezuela on the war.

Gómez was so angered, he claimed, that after one of Gómez's emissaries returned after talking with the Venezuelan minister in Washington, "there followed immediately suppression of only pro-Ally newspapers in Venezuela and imprisonment of editors and numerous arrests for alleged political offenses. Organizations and members of harmless theosophical society imprisoned for expressing approval of the United States in the war."

McGoodwin reported that forty farmers from various sections had been ordered by Gómez officials to report in person to the presidential palace twice a day, which led to "terrorizing their respective communities."

Eight days before, a popular priest had been imprisoned for criticizing Gómez. McGoodwin reported that the priest died "under torture this morning." Pro-German newspapers, of which there were more than a half dozen, he said, all continued to publish.

15

UH-OH

By 1918, the Office of Naval Intelligence had assembled a worldwide list of enemy agents, spies, and subversives it considered to be wartime threats to the United States.

When a copy of the navy's *Confidential "List A" of Aliens and Suspects, 1918* arrived in Caracas, Clark learned that his efforts to avoid the attention of US military intelligence had failed badly. It was worse than he'd ever imagined.

There was the further embarrassment because Captain Wright had informed him about it.

The oversize bound book listed the suspects in alphabetical order, and it contained their addresses and countries of residence.

Clark came home to the Barnacle late one afternoon, expecting nothing more than another night of war talk, cocktails, and poker. Wright was there waiting for him.

He called Clark over to the dining table where the book sat. The title was clearly readable.

Not knowing what would come next, Clark felt tense. He did what he always did in such uncomfortable situations. He adopted an aloof, confident air. He raised his nose a bit as he looked up at Wright. Wright was a military man's military man. He was stiff, authoritative, and unyielding. Nothing humored the captain. Wright turned to a page he'd marked and dragged his finger down the page to Clark's name. Clark's eyes followed the finger to his name. He noticed that his address was listed as being the Dolge home: Apartado 79 on the Plaza Panteón. Not even the navy's senior military intelligence officers knew that he had moved in with Wright.

Wright turned another few pages to show Clark the listings for Dolge and his wife. Dolge's address was listed as 2847 May Street, Cincinnati, Ohio. Mrs. Dolge was shown to reside at Apartado 79 on the Plaza Panteón.

Wright flipped another few pages to point out that the list also included Gómez.

Shocked by Wright's news, Clark forced himself to relax. He concentrated on breathing deeply and slowly. He desperately wanted to know more, but he was worried about appearing overly concerned to Wright.

However, he was pleasantly surprised by Wright's reaction. The captain made light of the list, assuring Clark that everyone knew that the list was badly flawed. He told Clark he'd nothing to fear. He wasn't aware, of course, of Clark's criminal past and his flight from New York.

He told Clark that he didn't intend to spread around the names beyond his own network of agents in Venezuela. He had no reason to, and he intended to keep the book at the Barnacle.

There were three reasons that Clark was listed. He had written newspaper articles defending the dictator and his war policies. Furthermore, Clark had a personal relationship with the dictator and the senior members of his cabinet. Lastly, Clark had a ten-year friendship with Dolge.

In his press articles, Clark reflected his own public position that Gómez was a friend of the United States. He consistently voiced this opinion to Andrade, who outlined the articles before contracting with Clark to write them. At the moment, the position taken by Andrade wasn't shared at the State Department, where the Margarita revelations and McGoodwin had poisoned opinion against Gómez.

Aware that McGoodwin was hammering him at the State Department, Clark retaliated, using his exposure to Wright to convince him that McGoodwin's ineptness and constant admonishments of Gómez were responsible for the dictator distancing his country from US policies on the war. He knew that Wright didn't like McGoodwin and that Wright could be influenced to blame the minister for the differences between the two countries.

Wright had been aware of Dolge's presence on the list before receiving it. He was likely responsible for its presence. He'd considered Dolge disloyal to the Allied cause since the captain had arrived in Venezuela the year before. Again, he advised Clark to maintain his distance from Dolge.

United States Navy and United States Army intelligence started gathering information on the Dolges in November 1917, tracking their travel in and out of Caracas, the United States, and Mexico.

The files noted Rudolf's loyalty to Germany, his friendship with the German minister in Caracas, and his frequent visits to the German legation house in Caracas.

In July 1917, naval intelligence reported on Dolge to the navy's chief investigator. They noted that Dolge had been in the United States frequently over the previous two years, spending his time with the "suspicious Wurlitzer people" in Cincinnati. The report noted that after Dolge's last trip to the United States, he'd returned to Caracas in November or December 1917. They noted that he was "very loud in his denunciation of the United States, stating publicly in the Venezuelan Club in Caracas before Venezuelans and Americans that the United States had gone into this war as the tool of England, that he'd been in Washington and knew that every department of the government was being run by a British officer, and that the president was a mere cat's paw for England. He further stated that he hoped the Germans would lick the British off the face of the earth, but of course as an American he wanted the Americans to lick the Germans."

Much of the information about Dolge's comments was supplied by Wright. Navy intelligence simultaneously shared it with the US attorney general and senior officials of the State Department.

The report was first circulated among US intelligence offices after Dolge sent letters from Mexico to his wife, his mother, a schoolteacher, and his banker. A postal censor in Laredo, Texas, intercepted the letters.

A report from the Office of Postal Censor indicated that a censor had opened the letters on November 9. To censor twenty-two, the description of the letters appeared to be innocuous. Postal censors had distributed the report for the following three reasons:

1. Writer is intimate friend of Herbert Bigelow of Cincinnati.
2. Because writer is in employ of Howard Wurlitzer (who is closely watched by Cincinnati police.)
3. Because writer is to be sent by Wurlitzer to Venezuela.

At the bottom of the file, it noted that the "German letter indicates that writer is hostile to German militarism." That letter was a ploy on the part of Dolge. He was hoping to convince censors that he was less supportive of Germany than he appeared to be. Dolge wrote a series of similar letters to his wife. He meant to suggest that he was loyal only to the United States. He carried copies of these letters with him in the event that he was searched. By then Dolge knew that his mail was being censored, and he was careful not to criticize the United States over the war. However, he'd not been as careful with his public remarks to others.

Bigelow, a Socialist and pacifist leader of the People's Church in Cincinnati, had recently been in the newspapers. After a prayer for the Kaiser and "the proud men surrounding him," Bigelow was abducted by local citizens and taken across the Ohio River to Florence, Kentucky, where he was tied to a tree and horsewhipped.

In another report to the US Bureau of Investigation, United States Army intelligence officers requested data on Dolge. The department explained that the Wurlitzer Music Company employed him as the chief of foreign sales. In this report, they also noted Wurlitzer's reputation as a leader of pro-German activities in Cincinnati.

In the summer of 1918, word was being passed through intelligence agencies that Dolge was about to travel again to Mexico for the Wurlitzer company. The Zimmermann affair had made Mexico a flashpoint in US intelligence circles.

When Captain Wright learned in June of the scheduled trip, he contacted navy intelligence to inform them that he was suggesting to the State Department that Dolge's passport be withdrawn. He told the navy that if Dolge was already en route to Mexico, he should be stopped at the border. Wright also told the navy that the

Passport Division at the State Department did not want Dolge to travel to Mexico.

Wright called the ostensible purpose of the trip, representing the Wurlitzer company, a ruse. He said that the Wurlitzers must have known that Dolge "has made an absolute failure of every commercial venture he ever went into." Wright charged that the real purpose of the trip was to "carry on German propaganda."

It eventually turned out that Dolge had a business reason for the trip.

Dolge had stopped in Cincinnati before traveling to Mexico. An ONI officer interviewed him and Howard Wurlitzer about the company's exporting of materials to South America that were not related to their music business, including soap, automobiles, trucks, and cotton goods.

Showing no alarm, Howard Wurlitzer explained to the agent that since the United States had entered the war, the company had received numerous orders for materials that were not related to music. The war, he said, had caused business disruptions.

Despite Wright's efforts, Dolge received a passport and traveled to Mexico. MID, the US Military Intelligence Division of the army, requested a report on the visit. The request called Howard Wurlitzer the "leader, spiritual, financial, and social, of the Germans and disloyalists in Cincinnati. What he would do for Germany is only limited by his fear of punishment. He is a very dangerous man."

After Dolge's telegrams were intercepted in Laredo, the captain of the army Signal Corps wrote that Dolge, who by then had returned from a recent trip to Mexico, had traveled with an American passport. He said that Dolge carried letters of introduction from the chief of the State Department's Consular Services.

He had other letters as well, including a letter of introduction to US Ambassador Henry P. Fletcher in Mexico.

The report went on to note that Dolge consistently traded with blacklisted German firms, and he had stated publicly that he would continue to do so.

Meanwhile, Clark had turned on his friend completely by attempting to portray Dolge as being disloyal.

He persuaded his coconspirator, Dr. Stewart, to join him in sending a cable to the State Department's Bureau of Citizenship to raise suspicion about Dolge. He hoped that his act would appear to be patriotic. Both of the men signed the cable. The bureau's chief, Roy Flournoy, passed the cable along to Carr at Consular Services, writing on it:

> Here is another telegram about Dolge. Have you the previous correspondence? I saw a statement recently that Clark is under suspicion. If I am not mistaken, Clark is the man in whose care Dolge left his laundry business when he departed from Caracas. I do not know who Stewart is or how much credence can be given to his statements.
>
> As I have observed before, Dolge's letters to his wife prove his entire loyalty to the country and his opposition to Germany absolutely, unless the copies, which he carried, were mere fabrications.
>
> Therefore, I am still of the belief that Dolge is all right.

In the left margin of the memorandum, Carr had scribbled "yes" to the question about the laundry being run by Clark when

Dolge was away. He also confirmed that Stewart was the US public health surgeon.

Before the United States entered the war, the pro-German, anti-British Dolges stridently eroded their friendships with others in the US colony in Caracas.

When the United States entered the war, many German-Americans immediately pledged their loyalties to the United States. Dolge was a politically unsophisticated man. He grew more vehement in his criticisms, and people frequently overheard him saying that the United States was too heavily influenced and taken in by England.

Although Mrs. Dolge and Alfred, Rudolf's father, were both born in Germany, the Dolge family was an American story. It was unfortunate that Rudolf couldn't have restrained his outrage over the war earlier.

Dolge had first come to Caracas in 1897 to open a warehouse of US goods for the National Association of Manufacturers. He opened his Americana Steam Laundry in Caracas, and he worked for the Orinoco Company. Because of Orinoco's role in financing the Matos Revolution, Dolge became ensnarled for decades in litigation with the Venezuelan government. Later, he would become a managing representative for Standard Oil in Venezuela. As years passed and his war positions were forgotten, he came to be known as the dean of the US colony in the country. To this day, his name is highly respected there.

Dolge's father had come to the United States in 1866, and he entered the piano felt business in New York.

In 1874, he discovered an abandoned tannery in Brockett's Bridge in the Adirondacks area of New York State. He bought it and set out to create a piano felt business in the United States, as well as a community to serve the citizens of Herkimer County.

Alfred was far ahead of his time. In 1876, he began a pension plan for his employees. In 1890, his employees received health insurance that the company paid for. Decades later, he found himself under investigation as an agent of Germany, as the US military solicited "detrimental information" on various members of the Dolge family and their businesses in the northeastern United States. The military found no detrimental information. Eventually, the town where his family established its business came to be named Dolgeville.

In October, one month before the armistice, US military intelligence learned that Anita Dolge and her son Alfred were leaving Venezuela for the United States. New York Police Sergeant Louis Morra approached the ship and stopped the Dolges on the pier. Among other things, he asked them about their reasons for coming to the United States. In Morra's passenger arrival report, he stated:

Subject: ANITA DOLGE and son, ALFRED DOLGE.

1: Subject arrived at this port from Venezuela on the SS *Philadelphia* of the Red D Line. She was reported by the purser of the ship as being a German and that her husband Rudolf Dolge, now in Mexico City, has been under suspicion of being a German agent for the past three years.

2: Subject stated that she was born in Germany on March 13, 1870, and came to the United States in 1893. In 1897, she said she went to Caracas, Venezuela, where she resided until 1918, when she left on account of her health. Mr. Dolge Sr. was born in New York City, December 13, 1869. He went to Venezuela, where he has been conducting the *Lavandería Americana,* located at Avenida Sur, Caracas, with residence at Plaza del Panteón No. 3, Caracas.

3: Mrs. Dolge stated further that her husband went to Mexico a few months ago for the Rudolf Wurlitzer Musical Instrument Company of Cincinnati. Dolge's parents were born in Germany, though he is an American citizen.

4: Alfred Dolge is coming to the United States for his military service.

They gave as a future address 629 Lincoln Avenue, Cincinnati.

Three days after arriving in New York with his mother, Alfred registered for the draft at Local Board 23 in Brooklyn. He was never able to serve.

He died in Brooklyn at the St. George Hotel on October 25, 1918. He died only eighteen days after returning to his native country. He was twenty-four years old. He had been under the care of a doctor for five days for bronchial pneumonia. He was yet another victim of the global flu epidemic.

16

THE OIL BUSINESS

O ne month before his sixty-second birthday, the chameleon
started a new career.

The general manager of the Caribbean Petroleum Co. in
Caracas, an American named Lewis Proctor, needed a sales
manager to begin exploring future outlets for the company's
oil products. In his fifth year as CPC's attorney in Caracas,
Doyle recommended Clark.

Proctor had past ties with the State Department. He was the
first of several former State Department officers to work on the
development of the oil industry in Venezuela.

Clark began his new job on April 1, 1918.

At the time, Venezuela's oil development was fraught with
competing interests. To help pay off foreign debt and to collect
concession payoffs from foreign companies, Gómez sought to
increase exploration. He pressured the local officers of the for-
eign-owned firms for expansion. After becoming convinced that
British capital held a complete monopoly on the production of
Venezuelan oil, he fostered competition.

The US oil companies became aware of the monopoly, but it
took them awhile. Misled by former officers who were working

for British oil interests, the State Department was even slower to recognize a monopoly, and proved to be of little help. In 1917, the US companies began working to reverse it.

The other major obstacle to increased production was the *barra*, a giant sandbar at the Maracaibo Harbor entrance. It limited the amount of oil that could be brought out of the oil region. Gómez wanted more oil sales, but he didn't want the bar to be removed. In their efforts to expand, CPC constructed pipelines and acquired a fleet of shallow draft boats that could clear the bar.

Clark again had high hopes for a concession to remove the bar. Clark was unaware that Gómez feared that by removing the bar a foreign warship might enter the harbor. Clark thought that the position with CPC could only enhance his chances. Regardless, the job was a godsend.

CPC staffed the company mostly with US citizens, including its top managers. Guided by Proctor, the managers helped bolster the myth that people from the United States owned the company. Its international game of hide-and-seek was continuing when Clark joined the company. Five years earlier, CPC's former US parent company, General Asphalt, informed its stockholders in its 1913 annual report that CPC had been sold to Royal Dutch Shell, which it plainly stated was British-owned.

This fact didn't become generally known or accepted at the State Department, however, and the company's central office in the Land Title Building in Philadelphia was cited as proof that CPC remained a US company.

Even after the State Department learned about the sale, it periodically launched full-fledged investigations of CPC ownership as late as 1929.

CPC's concession covered vast tracts of land in twelve Venezuelan states and the Territory of the Delta of the Orinoco.

In 1912, the company had brought in the leading US geologists at the time, including the eminent Ralph Arnold, to explore the land that was covered in the lease. General Asphalt concluded that the reserves were so large that the company lacked the resources to exploit them. Instead, the company approached Chairman Sir Henri Deterding of Royal Dutch Shell. Deterding decided to purchase controlling shares of CPC. Shell became a monopoly. It had controlling shares in all three of Venezuela's burgeoning oil companies.

Unsurprisingly, the State Department was confused in 1918. CPC's managers were using McGoodwin as their chief foil. Doyle in particular had great influence over McGoodwin, and he convinced him that the company was based out of the United States because its central address was listed in Philadelphia.

In his dispatches to the State Department in 1914, McGoodwin had boasted that CPC had struck oil on the eastern coast of Lake Maracaibo. With no thought that it was a British advance, he showed no concern, calling it the "first producing oil well in Venezuela." The well produced ten barrels a day, he said, and it produced high-grade oil. It was only the start of firsts that CPC would claim in Venezuelan oil development.

McGoodwin began his 1916 annual report on the oil industry with CPC one of six petroleum companies that were then working in oil exploration in Venezuela.

CPC was advancing faster than the other companies, and it had prepared sections for drilling on each side of Lake Maracaibo. On the eastern side of the lake, the company constructed a road and erected houses for its employees. In 1914, the company had shipped equipment for three wells, and begun drilling.

Assuming still that CPC was a US business, McGoodwin wrote that its San Lorenzo refinery, its pumping stations, and its pipeline would allow CPC to begin the first oil shipments by December 1916.

In 1917, the CPC juggernaut rolled up another first when it presented Gómez with the first drum of gasoline that was produced from Venezuelan oil. CPC distilled the gasoline at its refinery in San Lorenzo. British Minister Beaumont took note of the event. In his report to the Foreign Office in London, he referred to the company as "Caribbean Petroleum Co. of Philadelphia."

The job with CPC began another grand period for Clark. It was the first time in his ten years as an impostor that he had a regular and generous salary.

His work included traveling to Caribbean countries and islands and regularly contacting ministers, consuls, and oil executives, including Doyle.

Clark had maintained his friendship with Doyle. It hadn't led to the harbor-dredging project that he had wanted, but it had rewarded him with a job that elevated his income, security, prestige, and lifestyle. The position with CPC held promises of the better life he'd dreamed about for so long.

Writing of CPC hiring him, he told his children years later that from that point on, his life financially was "easy sledding."

North Americans living in Venezuela, especially those in the oil business, lived in a different world. They associated and socialized with the senior Venezuelan government officials, including Gómez. Because of their elevated positions in society, they had more accepting views of the dictator and his rule.

CPC maintained a house in Caracas of eighteen rooms at Salas a Caja de Agua No. 34 for its offices, where Proctor lived with his Venezuelan wife, his assorted maids, and employees who tended his garden.

The house was used for entertaining on a grand scale.

In the early years of oil exploration, the spare bedrooms of the house were frequently given over to important visitors, including Ralph Arnold and members of his family. At times, executives of the company lived there. Clark once spent weeks recuperating at the house after Doyle found him incapacitated on the floor of a bathroom.

Doyle insisted that he remain there, and he contracted a nurse to be with him.

As the war receded, Clark moved back into the Dolge residence. Any differences of opinion regarding the war were forgotten. The Dolges were sharing their home with two other boarders, Dr. Stewart and Henri Pittier. Pittier was a naturalist who was on loan from the US government to advise Venezuela on agriculture.

With the finances in better order, Clark began to entertain, and he reciprocated for the many invitations he had received over the years. Over Christmas of 1918, Clark hosted a holiday dinner for several American bachelors who had found themselves in Caracas without their families for the holiday. The Dolges were traveling outside of the country, and Clark had the run of the house.

Guests included Clark's housemates, Stewart and Pittier, and Doyle, as well as two other American oilmen, McKay and Edmund Griffiths. Griffiths was a consulting engineer with a US oil company, Carib Syndicate. The only South American there was the Argentine chargé d'affaires.

The center of attention for the evening was the noted naturalist and ornithologist George Kruck Cherrie, a skillful raconteur who entertained the men with tales of his service with the United States Naval Intelligence in Venezuela during the war.

As the night wore on, Cherrie began a long recitation of his expedition with Theodore and Kermit Roosevelt to the "River of

Doubt" in the Brazilian wilderness several years previous. The exploration cost the lives of several men in the party, including one who was murdered by another member of the expedition.

Clark would later relate Cherrie's account to his children in the United States. In his account, Cherrie described how everyone in the expedition nearly died from hunger, disease, and exposure. While the details of his account varied somewhat with other recorded accounts, Cherrie described how Roosevelt became so weak that he believed himself unable to survive. Roosevelt told Cherrie that he himself wouldn't live to get out, but he begged Cherrie to do all in his power to bring his son Kermit out safely.

Cherrie at once suspected that Roosevelt was aware of the lack of food remaining, and Roosevelt was contemplating either staying behind or committing suicide. Cherrie explained that he took up all the party's firearms and ammunition, and he kept them under his personal control. In Clark's account, he implied that the depravations that Roosevelt suffered on the trip were responsible eventually for his death.

Only a week after the dinner with Cherrie, on New Year's Day, 1919, Clark learned that a small French freighter named the *Marie Galante* was about to depart for a four-day trip to Fort de France, Martinique. With no notice, Clark rushed to La Guaira with suitcase in hand. Leaving only messages for Proctor and Doyle, he sailed out of the port early in the afternoon. He stopped only for long enough to purchase a deck chair for the trip.

He'd grown impatient because he wanted to show his associates that they had been smart to hire him. Steamship services outside the country had been limited for the war, and they hadn't resumed. Clark had dawdled for months. He had been unable to travel outside of the country to locate new outlets for CPC products.

Shortly after boarding the ship, Clark negotiated the captain out of his cabin near the freighter's bridge for a gold piece. Later in the afternoon, when he joined the captain and crew in the galley, he learned that his gold piece had also bought him the captain's place at the dinner table.

Taking his seat, Clark was surprised to learn that the daily food service began with a small glass of rum for each man. Claret and water were served with dinner. Luckily, the crew drank temperately.

With little to do during the days on the water, Clark sat in his chair on the deck and watched the crew as they trolled for fish off of the stern. The *Marie Galante* was dirty and ugly, but the food and the claret were better fare than he'd anticipated.

Clark carried letters of introduction that were addressed to the American consul at Martinique, Thomas Wallace. Clark had planned ahead. He had addressed letters to every US consul in the Caribbean during the slow months since his hiring. McGoodwin prepared one letter, and the French minister at Caracas prepared the other. The purpose of the letters went beyond introductions. Clark had no passport and he hoped to use the letters to gain entry into Martinique. It worked.

On arriving in Martinique, Clark took a room at the Grand Hotel de la Paix in Fort de France, and he looked up Wallace.

Life was good. He spent most of his time during his stay with Wallace, including having a dinner at the consul's home, where he was introduced to the other members of the North American colony.

He spent his afternoons with Wallace in the town plaza drinking tall tumblers of a rum and milk concoction with "small strips of dried vanilla plant." Clearly, he had more time than business required.

Clark signed up several future outlets for CPC products, and later he boasted to his children of the success of his ten-week trip.

While Clark was appreciative that Proctor had hired him, he knew that he really owed the job to Doyle. Proctor's penchant for being autocratic with Venezuelan officials and his associates at CPC had brought occasional problems. Clark used these problems to his advantage, frequently offering to intercede with Venezuelan government leaders when they took offense at Proctor's directness.

When Proctor retired, Doyle took over the management of all Royal Dutch Shell properties in the country. It was a substantial broadening of Proctor's responsibilities.

Relations between CPC and the government improved. Clark spoke favorably about Proctor, but he found in Doyle a shrewd man of great influence and cunning, with a mastery over various highly placed Venezuelan officials as he led the exploitation of oil in Venezuela.

"Efficient as the former had been," Clark recalled Proctor, "his ability was far surpassed by his successor. In addition to his training as a lawyer," Clark explained, Doyle's "unusual command of the Spanish tongue and his wide acquaintance with Latin America and its people" made him especially able as a business executive.

"He was possessed of the *suaviter in modo sed fortiter in re* needed to deal with Latins, and he had a grasp of the infinite details of our great business that made him easily the ablest among all managers of the oil industry within Venezuela.

"In addition to managing the Caribbean Co., he also managed the affiliated companies of the Royal Dutch Shell group, the Venezuelan Oil Concessions Ltd., and the Colon Development Co. Ltd. The three companies constituted the major petroleum interests in Venezuela, and they were the holders of vast areas that were under concessions from the government.

"The management of interests so vast and important and the retention of good relations with the constantly changing personnel of the government called for a man's-size personality and required all the energy of Doyle's six feet three and all the skill and diplomacy acquired during his varied career."

Clark's description of CPC, Colon, and the Venezuelan Oil Concessions companies was accurate. He did not, however, explain that Royal Dutch Shell was a British concern. He also did not explain that he, Doyle, and Proctor had conspired to mislead McGoodwin about who owned Royal Dutch Shell and CPC.

The world war had shown the importance of oil to navies. After questions about oil ownership in Venezuela were raised at the State Department and in military circles in Washington, McGoodwin was instructed to question CPC's senior officers.

Replying to a department inquiry, he reported that the CPC general manager "maintains that he is a salaried employee of the Caribbean Petroleum Co., an American corporation subsidiary of the General Asphalt Co. as he is also of the New York & Bermudez Co., also an American corporation and subsidiary of same; that he is in charge of development work and local sales and has (otherwise) no knowledge of the ownership."

Seven years had passed since CPC stock had been transferred to Shell, and the minister stumbled on as a true believer. Americans who were working for the British concerns had manipulated him.

Over the next two years, another player in the oil business made his presence felt.

McGoodwin informed Washington that the American McKay had offered $1,350,000 to Venezuela for the Colon concession, the British Controlled Oilfields concession, and the

Venezuelan Oil Concessions Limited. McKay, he said, offered Gómez the same amount of money as part of the deal, and he said that "very favorable prospects of acceptance" existed.

In Adee's response to McGoodwin, he had also noted McKay's aggressive involvement. He reported that he'd heard that "McKay had the Venezuelan government in the hollow of his hand."

Gómez declined McKay's offer.

Within a few weeks, feeling confident that the British oil monopoly in Venezuela had not been lost, Dormer wrote again to the Foreign Office. This time, he mentioned McKay. He told the Foreign Office that he believed that McKay was connected to Standard Oil. People who were familiar with the situation were saying that he had no "serious backing or connections and that his only object is to obtain concessions and sell them in the United States." Oddly, Dormer didn't consider him much of a threat.

"If rumor speaks true that 'he is here to make what he can and then clear out,' and that his exit will be an inglorious one, American interests as a whole will suffer a rude shock."

He then noted that McKay had developed close ties with a son-in-law and a brother of Gómez. The emergence of McKay and his growing influence with Gómez didn't impress Dormer, but this situation was creating the results that McKay and Clark had intended.

17

TOPPLING THE MINISTER

When McGoodwin arrived in Caracas for the first time in 1913, Clark was already serving as vice and deputy consul at La Guaira. McGoodwin quickly warmed to him, preferring his willing manner, high energy, and can-do spirit to consul Voetter's slow, wary pace and crusty, off-putting demeanor. The minister remained loyal to Clark throughout the consulate battles with Voetter and Brett, frequently informing Consular Services that he found Clark more capable than Voetter. But many things had eroded their friendship, including their differences during the war, Clark's associations with Wright and McKay, and Clark's fondness for William Phelps and his wife Alicia.

McGoodwin's downfall began with the allegations that he was accepting bribes from Gómez. These allegations came from every direction, and they came over a lengthy period of time. They came from Venezuelans, Americans, and other people from the diplomatic colony in Venezuela.

Even though there was no conclusive evidence for the rumors, US military intelligence copied the rumors in communiqués and routinely shared this information with the Office of the Counselor at the State Department.

Other US civilian personnel in Venezuela and supervisory personnel at the State Department also perpetuated the rumors. Supervisory personnel at the State Department in Washington even took seriously the allegations from López, the editor. Many came to believe the worst about McGoodwin, and many repeated the scurrilous charges surrounding him.

Among Venezuelan citizens, the views were founded in a belief that McGoodwin was supportive of Gómez with the State Department. The thinking was that if Washington understood the evil of Gómez, it would not allow the regime to remain in office. McGoodwin and his reports to the State Department must be misinforming the United States government about the dictator and his government. It was repeated by many in Venezuela that Gómez must be paying the minister to shade his reports.

Oddly, other than a brief period early in his posting, McGoodwin was consistently critical of Gómez and his dictatorship before, during, and immediately after the war.

That was beginning to change, however. McGoodwin would become strongly supportive of the dictator while partnering with him in business ventures. The partnership was publicly known after he became the minister, and some people voiced suspicions it was going on his last year as minister.

A report in 1918 to the Washington quarters of ONI was forwarded to Leland Harrison in the State Department's Office of the Counselor. This report quoted an intercepted letter from a Venezuelan exile in New York to Caracas. The author of the letter claimed that Gómez had paid ten thousand dollars to the American minister so that McGoodwin would deceive Washington and "neutralize" the ill feeling that the writer claimed that President Wilson harbored for Gómez.

According to Captain McCauley of ONI, the writer of the letter "says that Mr. McGoodwin must be treated with much amiability, as he's a wily one and knows a great deal, but not enough to deceive or alarm the Chief." The chief was Gómez.

In December of the same year, the director of the Office of Naval Intelligence wrote to the State Department to report that serious rumors about the American minister had surfaced "much to his detriment."

The report stated that while McGoodwin was believed to be "entirely loyal" in the war effort, a position that hadn't reached a consensus among the US military thanks to Captain Wright, he was thought not to be "strictly honest." The report described McGoodwin as not being strong enough to cope with all that lay ahead, and it said that American interests demanded a man of "greater ability."

The writer, Rear Admiral Roger Welles, was critical of the American civilian representation in Venezuela generally, and he stated that the US efforts with the Enemy Trading Act in Venezuela were neither zealous nor effective. He called the efforts a farce.

As early as 1919, McGoodwin was looking for a way out of Venezuela, and he was hoping that he would hold the title of minister.

He called on his old friend from Oklahoma, Scott Ferris, to approach the State Department to recommend him for another posting. Ferris was then representing Oklahoma as a congressman.

The State Department suggested Siam to Ferris. Ferris replied that McGoodwin was hopeful of something else. Siam was too far away. The move would be too expensive and impractical for his family. McGoodwin sought something that wasn't a "demotion,"

Ferris said. Nothing came of the request and McGoodwin remained in Caracas.

By 1920, the British legation in Caracas viewed McGoodwin as thoroughly damaged goods. The annual report for the year that went to the foreign secretary called his relations with Gómez "a mystery" that led to many unflattering rumors. The report added that it was difficult for anyone to cooperate with the American minister because of his "lack of straightforwardness of manner."

Looking ahead, Dormer, the British minister, anticipated his replacement, stating, "His departure, as that of his wife, will be hailed with general satisfaction."

Dormer noted that McGoodwin was "seldom seen in the morning."

Dormer concluded that Venezuela had succeeded in winning over McGoodwin through flattery and hospitality. He cited the unprecedented loan of the Federal Palace Capitol for a ball that McGoodwin was hosting to celebrate the Independence Day holidays of both the United States and Venezuela in July 1920.

The use of the palace was much talked about, the report said. In fact, the British minister reported to London that people in diplomatic circles frequently and cynically asked if Venezuela had become an American protectorate.

The report noted that when McGoodwin went on leave in September that year, Venezuelan loaned him a war vessel to transport his family to Puerto Cabello.

As McGoodwin embarked, the report stated, people overheard General Gómez saying, "Now he will do what I like." The story had wings. John Wiley of the US legation, at the time monitoring McGoodwin on directions from superiors at the State

Department, informed the secretary of state that Gómez actually said, "Now he will tell them I'm all right."

William Guillermo Sherwell, a language professor from Georgetown University who was in Venezuela with a group of students, gave credence to these accusations. Dr. Leo S. Rowe, an American who headed the Pan American Union, of which Sherwell was associated, passed Sherwell's eleven-page report, dated May 10, 1921, to Sumner Welles at the State Department. Sherwell's report was stunning in its denouncement of American representation in Caracas.

Sherwell depicted McGoodwin and Gómez as having an evil alliance in which they held Venezuelans hostage while keeping the United States blind to what was really going on in the country. Sherwell concluded that both men had to go.

Regarding the relationship between the minister and the dictator, Sherwell wrote: "They justify the fear that [McGoodwin] may misinform the government about the real kind of a man the general is."

Still, as time passed, McGoodwin somehow remained. His expected replacement hadn't materialized with the new administration. He let it be widely known that even with Republicans in power, his valuable presence was necessary in Caracas.

Then came the final, lethal blow. It originated with Mrs. McGoodwin.

McGoodwin had many enemies. After himself, his wife was his worst. Members of the diplomatic community in Caracas and Americans outside the legation recognized his wife's inexplicable persuasive power over him. He was defenseless against her powers, and her powers would bring an end to his diplomatic career.

He would tangle with William H. Phelps, who was considered the bulwark of US business in Venezuela.

The McGoodwins were hostile toward Phelps and his wife Alicia, and these hostilities had become well known to the US community around Caracas. The Americans attributed the origin of these hostilities to Mrs. McGoodwin's jealousy over the social and professional standing of Phelps and his wife.

For a second year in a row, Venezuela and the US colony in Caracas combined their celebrations of Independence Day in 1921. Venezuelan and US officials hosted the events. All of Venezuelan officialdom would take part, including Gómez and his family.

The United States began the celebration on the Fourth of July with a ball at McKay's expansive residence in Caracas. On the following day, the Venezuelan congress held a reception at the capitol.

Hours before McKay's ball was scheduled to begin, General Andrade called on Clark, informing him that the American minister and his wife were staying away from the ball because Phelps and his wife would be there. They also threatened to leave the Venezuelan event the next day if they appeared. It fell to Clark to resolve the matter.

Clark later wrote of the events in a diary for his children.

There was a most unpleasant incident. A serious feud had developed between Mr. McGoodwin, the American minister, and his wife on the one part, and Mr. and Mrs. Phelps, of our American colony, on the other.

The fault lay wholly with the former, but despite that, the minister and his wife refused to attend McKay's ball and threatened to leave the Congress Hall if Phelps and his wife attended.

At all hazard, we felt that a scandal must be avoided, and since the American government representative must be present, it fell to my lot, after conference, to persuade them not to attend either affair, at the same time assuring them of our confidence and our indignation at the McGoodwins' attitude.

Just after the holiday, McKay and Clark went to Phelps, urging him to go to Washington to file a complaint against McGoodwin. Phelps followed their advice and contacted his brother, Dudley F. Phelps, an attorney who was practicing in New York, to help him make his case.

After sending off several letters to Washington officials, including the president, Phelps left for the United States.

His letters, dated July 26, 1921, brought an instant response from the State Department. The department immediately agreed to see his brother, who preceded him to Washington.

On July 29, Robert Woods Bliss, the third assistant secretary at the State Department, wrote a memorandum. It began:

I received this afternoon Mr. Dudley F. Phelps, who was referred to me by the under secretary. Mr. Phelps showed me a copy of a letter which he had, addressed to the president, charging the American minister at Caracas with statements regarding Mr. [William] Phelps which would tend to hurt his business relations in Venezuela or make it necessary for him to close down entirely.

In answer to my question as to why he thought that the minister was endeavoring to discredit him with General Gómez, he replied that the matter undoubtedly grew out of the dislike Mrs. McGoodwin had for Mrs. Phelps, and that Mrs. McGoodwin dominated the minister so that he acted entirely under her influence and upon her every suggestion.

In the memorandum, Bliss explained that William Phelps had let pass Mrs. McGoodwin's dislike for Mrs. Phelps in social matters. However, now that "the minister had denounced him to Mr. Gómez," he felt that he had to respond to protect his business.

Bliss concluded:

> Mr. Phelps expressed his hope that the department would investigate the matter without delay, and felt sure that it would find that Mr. McGoodwin was not a proper person to represent the United States in a diplomatic capacity.

In his memorandum, Bliss noted that Dudley Phelps had handed him a copy of the letter, along with a list of American businessmen in Caracas "whom he knew would substantiate these charges against the minister."

The list included McKay, four managers of oil companies, four assistant managers of oil companies, the manager of a coffee company, and Charles Freeman, who had once been McGoodwin's close friend. At the time, Freeman was an agent for Gaston, Williams & Wigmore, Inc. of New York. Clark was included on the list.

Phelps added that McGoodwin's reason for refusing to attend the Fourth of July events if Phelps attended "was that I was an enemy of the Venezuelan government. General Gómez made the situation known to me through mutual friends." These mutual friends were Clark and McKay.

Phelps also addressed a letter to the secretary of state. He said that ever since Phelps departed Venezuela in July, he'd been informed that McGoodwin was "representing to General Gómez that I am responsible for the news items and editorials which have appeared in American newspapers derogatory to the Venezuelan government, and that my trip to the United States was for the purpose of carrying on this propaganda."

McGoodwin knew otherwise. In 1918, when McGoodwin was complaining to the State Department about Clark's articles, which glorified Gómez and misstated Venezuela's real position on the war, the State Department responded by asking who the regular correspondent for Associated Press was in Venezuela. At the time, McGoodwin responded that it was Phelps. McGoodwin remarked that stories by Phelps he found were fair and balanced.

Phelps said that he had been told that he wouldn't be allowed to return to Caracas because of "the activities of Mr. McGoodwin." That information came to Phelps from Clark. Andrade had approached Clark, and he had asked him to help bring the problem to a peaceful resolution.

Phelps denied any involvement in the latest newspaper articles. He stated that although he'd been a correspondent for the Associated Press for fourteen years, he was involved with no specific newspaper. His communications with the Associated Press had always been limited to cable messages filed "in plain English, all of which subsequently were examined and passed by the cable censor of the Venezuelan government."

Phelps had come to Venezuela to live fulltime in 1897. Early on, he worked for the US legation and, in addition to his work for Associated Press, was an occasional correspondent for the *New York Tribune.* He had met Alicia Elvira Tucker, whose family had settled in Venezuela from England, and married her.

Phelps had graduated from Harvard. He became interested in ornithology and organized expeditions in Venezuela and wrote books about the expeditions and various bird species, many of which he discovered. He built a huge business enterprise at the same time, amassing what US officials believed to be two hundred thousand dollars.

One son, known as Billy, took up his father's interest and they collaborated on many ornithology projects and publications. His son eventually donated his vast collection of bird specimens to the Museum of Natural History.

Phelps Sr. was too important, too well liked, and too respected. McGoodwin had been foolish with his wild accusations.

McGoodwin learned of his own resignation in a telegram from the secretary of state on September 24, 1921. Marked "confidential for the Minister," the telegraph explained that the resignation of a chief of a diplomatic mission was "always in the hands of the executive. The president has directed me to inform you of the acceptance of your resignation of the post of Envoy Extraordinary and Minister Plenipotentiary to Venezuela."

Secretary of State Charles Hughes signed the telegram. He informed McGoodwin that his successor was Willis C. Cook. He instructed McGoodwin to obtain the approval of Cook from the Venezuelan government as soon as possible. In noting Cook's background, he pointed out that Cook too was a newspaperman. Cook was the owner and publisher of the *Sioux Falls Daily Press*.

On October 6, Henry Fletcher sent Phelps a letter. Fletcher was now an assistant to Hughes. He informed Phelps, "For your information, it may be stated that the president has sent the nomination of Willis C. Cook of South Dakota as minister to Venezuela."

Fletcher followed up the next day with a letter to McGoodwin, instructing McGoodwin to arrange to see Gómez and correct the impression that Gómez had of Phelps.

He was too late.

Wasting no time, McGoodwin informed the department on October 5 that he was leaving Caracas for the United States that day aboard the steamship *Caracas*. He informed the department that legation secretary White "will present the name of successor."

In Clark's account of his own role in the imbroglio, he wrote, "McKay and I advised Mr. Phelps to go at once to Washington and prefer formal complaint of the minister's action, for in effect this was an attack affecting the business standing of the leading American merchant in Venezuela. Mr. Harding was president and Mr. Hughes, the secretary of state. We gave Phelps letters confirming his statements. He followed our counsel, preferred complaint to the secretary of state, and in October following McGoodwin was recalled."

Writing of the McGoodwins, Clark said that he had worked to maintain good relations with the couple, but they never became intimate.

"The lady was extremely erratic, to state it mildly. When the feud came about between her and Mrs. Phelps, she suggested to me that I could not be a friend of hers and of Mrs. Phelps at the same time. I made it plain to her that, if such were the case, I should have to sacrifice her friendship, for Mrs. Phelps was my very old friend and one whom I greatly respected.

"It was brought to me later, by a woman friend, that Mrs. McGoodwin related my statement to another woman who was somewhat of a toady to her, and that this woman expressed her sympathy by saying that Mr. Clark was *un viejo intrigante*, an intriguing old fellow. I said that I had no objection to being called intriguing, but that I did resent being called old."

Not long afterward, Wiley, the former legation secretary who by then had been assigned to the division of Western European Affairs in Washington, received two letters there from Freeman in Caracas.

Freeman said, "For the government people here it was rather a shock when they heard of the appointment of Mr. [Willis] Cook as minister here, because they believed firmly that McGoodwin would return. He surely could make them believe anything," Freeman wrote.

Freeman counseled Wiley that "No man in Venezuela is more hated and despised by natives and foreigners than Mr. McG. His acquiescence to the unscrupulous conduct of his wife is something nobody can understand. Their only object seems to be to keep in the good graces of Gómez and his bastard children and they are not ashamed of any act, however low and cringing, as long as they get a chance to publicly proclaim the 'greatness' of Gómez. She has gone so far as to threaten Venezuelan ladies, who did not like the idea of going to a picnic to Maracay with telling the general that they were not friends of the administration, and this is the American minister and his wife!"

Freeman alluded to the common belief that McGoodwin was accepting graft.

"Of course you can't blame the natives here for believing that McG. is in the pay of Gómez, considering everything that has passed here. As I know McG, he is the most unscrupulous liar who would not hesitate at anything. To quote his wife in a conversation with me, when I was persona grata, 'He is the biggest liar and will double-cross his best friend; don't ever believe a word he says.' That is the opinion his own wife has of him."

18

ALL THE PRESIDENT'S MEN

After the war, Captain Wright gave up the Barnacle and prepared to leave Venezuela. McKay moved into the sprawling home in Caracas and asked Clark to join him. They both saw an opportunity.

Through the winters and into summers of 1920, 1921, and 1922, the two men hosted what would become known as "McKay's Sunday Night Dinners." The guest lists read like a Who's Who in Caracas. It included the American minister and his wife, the US military attachés, and high officials of the Venezuelan government. Dr. Rafael Requena and his wife were always in attendance.

As he frequently did, Clark kept lists of all who attended. He took the time to draw the shape of the table and to show where each guest sat.

McKay was always at the head of the table, and sometimes Clark joined him. At other times, Clark removed himself to the foot of the table or he sat on the side, making way for a guest who was being specially honored.

Mr. and Mrs. Phelps frequently sat at the table. Once, they sat with the McGoodwins before the minister was recalled. Less frequent guests included British Minister Beaumont, his wife, and several of Clark's associates at CPC.

The long table comfortably accommodated as many as twenty-five guests.

On his arrival in Venezuela, McKay lacked an introduction into the US diplomatic and business communities, and he also lacked an introduction to Venezuelan government officials. These things Clark provided, steering McKay first to Dr. Requena, Gómez's personal secretary and primary liaison between Gómez and those with whom he had business, and then to Gómez himself.

Over the years, Clark has made many efforts to get to know Gómez, and these efforts were at last showing promise. He was among the few Americans who had been invited to visit the Gómez residence at Maracay. He photographed Gómez, Requena, and Gómez's brother Juan Crisóstomo Gómez, who was known as Don Juancho. They were relaxing in lawn chairs under the shade of huge trees on the estate's grounds.

At one dinner at McKay's house, three Americans sat at the head of the table: Clark, McKay, and Fred Hall Kay. The three men had begun to discuss how best to exploit their mutual interests and resources, including their collective influence with Gómez, which was becoming substantial.

They had brought in a fourth man, who sat along one side of the table. Señor Juan M. Rodríguez González, a Venezuelan lawyer and a relative of Requena, had joined the conversation. In 1921, both McKay and McGoodwin met with Gómez to press for changes in the oil laws, many of which ended up being adopted. In 1922, when the companies pushed for additional changes and refinements, McKay and Hall were both instrumental in redrafting the codes.

McKay represented Sun Oil and Standard Oil of New Jersey. Kay represented Venezuelan Sun Ltd. and Venezuelan Oilfields Co. Ltd., to which he'd already transferred concessions.

McKay's unsuccessful bid for the big British concessions of CDC, VOC, and British Controlled Oilfields was a disappointment. While the three British concessions were revalidated, however, McKay was successful for Sun Oil, negotiating five concessions from Requena and Don Jauncho in Trujillo State.

Since McKay was successful in opening oil exploration to US companies, US military intelligence in Washington and Venezuela wanted to know more about him. In 1921, they requested a full report on his earlier business activities in Mexico and Guatemala.

What came back from the US military attaché in Mexico City was shocking.

The attaché's report indicated that McKay had first come to MID's attention in Mexico in 1907. This report portrayed a clever, ruthless, and sinister businessman who was "self-assured" and "self-reliant." He was regarded "as a thorough going 'sport,' ready to gamble on any hazard and exceedingly successful with the 'ladies.'"

He was described by one source, a prominent Mexican businessman, as "thoroughly unscrupulous."

In Mexico, he worked with the Southern Pacific Railroad. He dealt with railway operations and oil interests. McKay served as the personal representative of the vice president.

In 1909, he acquired an interest in the Mercantile Bank in Mexico City, but by 1910 or early 1911 his service as president ceased. The report didn't explain how he came to buy the interest, but it noted that he was associated with Mexico's vice president. Calling McKay "a man of no financial standing," the report claimed that he left behind many debts, and he owed Mercantile Bank two hundred thousand dollars. The report attributed his debts to his "gambling propensities."

When McKay was "let out" in 1912 by Southern Pacific for reasons unknown, he left Mexico, but he returned in 1914 to the Tampico district and showed an interest in the oil business there.

As questionable and troubled as his background in Mexico was portrayed, McKay's alleged activities in Guatemala were even darker. US military intelligence concluded that he'd promoted a revolution against the government of President Manuel José Estrada Cabrera.

When his attempt failed, a coconspirator named Bonillas, who claimed he was working with McKay, charged that McKay had tricked him out of forty thousand dollars. This was his share of money for his role in the revolution. Bonnillas was found murdered in Mexico City under circumstances that were "never cleared up," according to the report of MID Colonel Harvey Miller.

McKay had come to Venezuela in 1917. This raised the hackles of the US minister, who feared he was after his job. However, McKay indicated that he was interested in buying copper mines.

US military intelligence saw Requena as Clark's main entrée to Gómez, and Gómez had just appointed Requena to oversee the country's business development. Requena held several government positions over many years. He was a doctor. Many years before, he had treated Gómez for a battle wound when Gómez led the armies of Castro.

Various Gómez family members, including his brother and two sons-in-law, were already involved in oil development and concessions.

It was perfect timing for McKay. His meteoric ascendancy in the oil business had resulted from his association with Requena. By some accounts, he'd become an informal counselor to the dictator by 1920. By 1921, the dictator made no decisions about the oil industry without his counsel. Requena was also involved in the drafting of the country's petroleum laws.

Clark had been building his entrée with Gómez and the Venezuelan government for many years, but in 1921 he organized a huge celebration to honor the founding fathers of the United States and Venezuela.

The crowning moment of the celebration was the unveiling of a monument of Bolívar in New York's Central Park. A simultaneous ceremony was staged in Caracas, where a statue of George Washington was moved from its location next to the Municipal Theater to a prominent residential portion of Caracas called El Paraíso.

The entire officialdom of Caracas turned out for the event, including Gómez, who was seated prominently in the middle of the front row of about twenty-five of his top army commanders. All of them were in uniform. Dr. Márquez Bustillos sat prominently nearby with a separate large group that included the Venezuelan cabinet. All of them were dressed in long black formal coats, and they all wore top hats. The National Congress was there as well.

Behind the two groups stood hundreds of onlookers.

On the following day, the press of Caracas printed the entire dedication speech of the American Committee, which had planned the dual celebrations. The speech, in Caracas, was presented by Clark, chairman of the committee, which included Doyle, Kay, Robert P. Holt, and Eric V. Juce. Clark gave his speech in Spanish. He saluted the "mutual sympathy and the harmony of international relations which exist between these two American republics."

Clark called to the attention of his Venezuelan audience that both presidents, Gómez and Harding, were taking part in the simultaneous ceremonies.

"In New York, President Harding, your own accomplished minister of Foreign Affairs, and the American secretary of state testify by their presence to the admiration which all Americans and lovers of liberty share with you for the fame and work of the great South American Liberator, Bolívar, and here in the capital of Venezuela the cooperation of General Gómez, of your cultured provisional president, and the distinguished representative of the government of the United States testify in like manner to the reverence with which free peoples cherish the name and fame of George Washington."

Landis, the US military attaché at the time, described the ceremony as "impressive as could be staged here, but throughout partook more of the nature of a laudation of General Gómez and his regime than of Washington."

He called the combined one of a "series of efforts on the part of the Gómez regime to pull the wool over the eyes of the American government as to their pronouncedly pro-German attitude during the world war and to the local political conditions here at present and to further use the much advertised friendship of the United States, in the first place to discourage revolutionary movements here and abroad and, second, to give the impression that the United States looks with favor upon local political conditions, those existing now and which have existed during the past twelve years."

Landis continued by saying, "In both of the above, they have probably succeeded, as it is doubtful whether the new American president or secretary of state are more than superficially advised as to present and past conditions in this country."

Throughout the reign of Gómez, Americans found ways to help the dictator. Through their efforts, they often enriched themselves and those they represented. Doyle and the US oilmen liked the stability that the dictator brought to the country, and they found it easier to deal with one man, usually at his Maracay residence. The US oil community in the country was willing to lend its public support to Gómez.

Under the heading "Action of American Oil Representatives in Support of Gómez Government," a military attaché complained of a letter that had appeared on the front page of *El Universal* in Caracas in 1923.

The article described "praise and sympathy for the order established by Gómez." Below this article were the signatures of five Americans working for American oil companies at Maracaibo. The statement criticized elements that were trying to interrupt commerce in the country. These interruptions obviously went against the interests of the companies.

The military attaché concluded that the oilmen's acquiescence in the publishing of the statement was a mistake. He wrote that it was to the "ultimate interest" of the United States to remain neutral in all political activities in Venezuela. To do otherwise, he said, would encourage anti-American feelings in the country.

He said that things like the letter led to the common complaint that the United States was helping support Gómez for purely commercial self-interest. Meanwhile, Gómez was "so sorely oppressing and exploiting the people of the country."

Another American was preparing to join the developing oil business in Venezuela. McGoodwin had been away for only four months.

Word of his imminent return came to Washington from the new US military attaché, Major Cary Crockett. Reporting to MID from Caracas in February 1922, Crockett doubted that McGoodwin's arrival would be advantageous to the American legation. Speaking of McGoodwin, Crockett said, "His reputation here is bad."

In McGoodwin's waning days as minister in Caracas, Márquez Bustillos wrote to Gómez, urging him to make use of the "good friendship" that he had developed with McGoodwin and to engage him in active propaganda against Gómez's opponents in the United States. Bustillos mysteriously added that Gómez should do this "while holding hands with the person or the agent of whom I spoke to you in my other letter."

He added, "The acquisition of a person such as Mr. McGoodwin fighting in our favor would be an effective value, and it could help dissipate that atmosphere of lies and slander with which we are attacked."

McGoodwin signed on.

There were many opinions about the precise moment when Gómez began to court McGoodwin, but the relationship was warm and cooperative by the time McGoodwin was recalled.

Early in 1920, the minister invited McGoodwin and his wife to spend a week in Maracay in the spring. In June, the minister called on Gil Borges to inform him that he was taking his annual leave and he planned to use the "opportunity to relate the work of national reconstruction" made by the dictator. McGoodwin told Borges that he also planned to "put in the light your (Gómez) personality and good deeds."

McGoodwin asked Gómez for "twelve to fifteen" of his "best photographs, if possible etched in steel, to reproduce in the American press."

Later, after he returned to the United States, McGoodwin let the general know that he was faithfully working on the job. He wrote to him that he was keeping a close eye on his enemies who were operating in New York, and he was countering lies about Gómez and Venezuela that were appearing in the US press. In his letters, which he wrote from the Waldorf Astoria Hotel in New York, McGoodwin informed the dictator that he expected to return to Venezuela within weeks. He explained that he'd been offered the presidency of an oil company that was planning to develop petroleum around Lake Maracaibo.

McGoodwin told Gómez that López Bustamante, "who has his propaganda offices in 274 Canal Road and his residence at 1015 Trinity Avenue of this city, has written a letter to the newspaper *The World,* published in this city, explaining that Mr. Cook 'has been duly counseled about the political situation in Venezuela,' and that he won't be fooled by the Lone Boss (meaning Gómez), better said, and using uglier terminology, as the idiot McGoodwin has been fooled. López Bustamante, [Manuel Antonio] Pulido [Méndez], etc., have been very busy suggesting things to Mr. Cook, but the newspapers of this city have refused to publish their communiqués."

McGoodwin was implying that he was responsible for keeping the anti-Gómez opposition and their comments to the new US minister out of the newspapers in New York.

A month later, he wrote to declare his date of arrival and to announce his appointment as president of Creole Development Company's division, Lago Petroleum Co. Crockett informed MID that McGoodwin would be paid twenty-five thousand dollars a year.

"I'll have the pleasure of going to live in Venezuela for about five years," McGoodwin told Gómez. "If you want me to be frank, I wish I could live there forever."

He then asked the dictator to look after his household goods, which he was sending ahead. He asked the "Chief to order those in charge to ease the entry of the luggage."

In June 1922, the payoff for Clark's years of patronizing Gómez finally came. McKay, Clark, and Kay formed a corporation with Rodríguez, the Venezuelan attorney. The sole purpose of the corporation was to protect the Gómez fortunes and to promote his business interests.

Notice of the partnership was published in the *Boletín de la Bolsa,* a financial publication in Caracas, which reported the breadth and governance of the corporation. McKay, Kay, and Clark each invested five thousand bolivars to form the company.

McKay was listed as manager, and Clark and Rodríguez were listed as assistant managers. They formed a second corporation simultaneously. The publication also listed McKay as the manager, and Clark and Rodríguez assistant managers. Each partner put up one thousand bolivars. The report noted Clark's lengthy residence in Caracas, his position with the Caribbean Petroleum Co., and his service to McKay as his secretary and representative.

Under certain circumstances, the corporations were to take over and place the Gómez fortunes under American protection. This included the "states and properties of all description acquired by General Gómez and the relatives and associates during Gómez's rule as dictator."

The corporations were also the means to manage Gómez's businesses and concessions, including the sale of oil concessions and other mining enterprises. One company would focus on acquisition and transport, including rail, real estate, oil, concessions, banking, electric power, and coal. The second company was intended to establish branches in New York City and elsewhere to dispose of the properties.

Gómez and his partners also intended to control retail, manufacturing, transport, and import and export.

If Doyle or CPC, for whom Clark still worked, had concerns about a conflict of interest over Clark's relationship with McKay, Clark never alluded to it. By all accounts, Doyle was savvy enough to protect himself and CPC, and he probably didn't share everything he knew with Clark. Still, Clark naturally attempted to work both sides to his advantage.

McKay, meanwhile, was enjoying a significantly improved reputation with the US military representatives. After the original report on his alleged activities in Mexico and Guatemala, US military intelligence was grudgingly acknowledging by 1921 that he was having some success with US oil companies. In 1922, his influence became clear when Gómez instructed that a draft of the new petroleum law be turned over to McKay for his examination and "possible revision," before the Venezuelan congress approved it. Military attachés were soon speaking of McKay in reverential terms.

McKay's efforts on behalf of the dictator included undertaking secret missions for Gómez in the United States and lobbying the US government to use its influence to prevent armed interferences from the revolutionary movements in "France, Spain, Holland, or Germany."

MID reports began noting that McKay was able to influence Gómez because of the contact that McKay and Clark had with Dr. Requena. In a report from February 1921, Major Landis called Clark an "intimate friend" of Requena. In a report from 1923, Major Crockett noted that McKay "had made much money for the ruling family here in disposing of concessions."

By the middle of the 1920s, US military intelligence was extolling McKay for single-handedly breaking the British oil monopoly in Venezuela and opening the way for American development there.

Gómez had them all in his pockets, in his prisons, or in exile.

19

THISCLOSE

C lark's secret past remained undetected for a decade and a half, but in 1923 it almost caught up with him.

It wasn't the police in New York City. It'd been years since anyone at the Brooklyn Detectives Bureau had spent time searching for Henry Sanger Snow.

They'd long ago lost interest. Many of them had retired. Nothing they did brought them any closer to capturing him.

Neither Anna nor the children knew it, but there was a period of close surveillance from 1909 to 1914 that included an American detective following them to Europe in 1909. He hid his real identity and took up residence as their neighbor in Switzerland. Ironically, it was the same year that Clark had returned to New York for the first time.

Five years after Snow's disappearance, an *Oakland Tribune* reporter brought the detective's surveillance to light. The reporter had learned from Brooklyn police that the futile hunt for Snow was drawing to a close. He journeyed to Chestnut Hill outside Philadelphia to observe how Mrs. Snow and her children were getting along. He described her as caring for her children and living with them in a well-to-do-suburb. He also spoke with various former friends of Snow in New York. He said that the abrupt turnaround in Snow's fortunes had left the "substantial men of Brooklyn" so aghast and bewildered that they still "refused to credit their hearing." They continued to believe that Snow was an innocent man.

In the gentlemen's clubs, which the reporter visited, one of the "substantials" had stood up to state in the reporter's presence, "Well, if Henry Sanger Snow was crooked, who can you trust?"

After interviewing Snow's former friends, the reporter became convinced that Snow had received help with avoiding police during his escape.

"The story of his escape bears out the supposition that they rallied to his aid. That Henry Sanger Snow, known to thousands in Brooklyn, could have gone scot-free, without the connivance of friends, is beyond the bounds of belief."

The detective who spied on Anna and the children in 1909 related a bittersweet moment that he had witnessed after covertly following Anna on foot to a mountain resort. He had hidden to observe her reading letters that she had pulled from a package with ribbons around it.

He told the Oakland reporter that he had watched as she opened some of them to read. She even kissed some of the letters. When she was through, she individually tore up each of them into tiny pieces, which she left on the ground.

When she walked away and was out of sight, the detective gathered the torn letters, one of which he was able to piece back together. As he told the newspaper reporter who was researching and writing about the case in 1914, the scraps contained "an old love message" from Henry Snow.

It was in Snow's love poems that he came closest to admitting his wrongdoings. These always contained only occasional and subtle language. Snow never used terms as embezzlement, crime, disappearance. One was addressed to Anna and entitled:

TO MY WIFE

I'm dreaming, Love, of all the years
We've journeyed arm in arm,
Sharing the laughter and the tears,
The joys and sorrows, hopes and fears,
The sunshine and the storm.

'Twas May-time when, with bridal wreath
Twined in thy red-gold hair,
Thou plightest me thy wifely troth
And gave, with all a woman's faith,
Thy life to my dear care.

To give thee love, Sweetheart, I've tried,
In a man's foolish way;
And if I've failed, forbear to chide,
For failure hath the love belied
That ne'er from thee could stray.

If I've brough tears, Sweet, to thine eyes
Or sorrow to thy heart,
Forgive, dear Love, the fault that cries
For pity; contrite, I would rise
To play the nobler part.

There's silver now amid the gold
That crowns thy cherished head;

But love, dear heart, that ne'er grows old,
Is sweeter, as the years unfold,
Than when we first were wed.

The detective learned nothing in the letter that would help him locate his quarry.

In Clark's earlier years in Venezuela, the two American consuls at La Guaira, Brett, and Voetter before him, voiced their suspicions about Clark and his nebulous past, although neither of them seemed to have probed very deeply. Their only real interest was to raise enough doubt to rule him out for work at the consulate.

George Marshall Allen and others in New York, as well as the Ponds in Venezuela, kept his secret and knew where he was. They continued to maintain contact, and in Allen's case he helped him remain at large with gifts of money. Everyone seemed to remain loyal.

Clark hadn't shared his secret with Doyle. While he related much about his illegal activities at the consulate to McGoodwin, he never breathed a word about his real secret. However, someone was talking.

The United States Army's military intelligence would come the closest to revealing Snow. While based as a military attaché in Caracas, Major Crockett devoted his entire monthly report on political conditions in Venezuela in December 1923 to Clark.

The major had been told the shadowy story. While lacking some details, the story did disclose the name of Snow.

Entitled "The Representative of the Associated Press at Caracas," the report began by noting that William Phelps had begun turning over his duties for the Associated Press to Norman C. Clark, whom Crockett described as "an American, about sixty-eight years of age, of good education, with an excellent knowledge of Spanish as well as English, and who has been occupied at Caracas in various kinds of work during the past twenty years."

His information was only slightly off. Clark had first arrived in Caracas fifteen years before, and he would turn sixty-eight the following May.

The report raised the topic of the threat of exposure in the fourth paragraph:

> It is alleged that he left the United States under a cloud and that he cannot return to his home; also that his real name is not Clark but Snow. He is a good writer and is the author of a historical novel published in the United States about twenty years ago, entitled *The Romance of St. Sacrement.*

How Crockett learned about Clark's real identity, his background, and his book remains a mystery. Clark had made a gift of the book to two women in Venezuela. Hettie Beaumont was the wife of the British minister, and Betty Moffat White was the wife of the US legation secretary and the daughter of Burnham Moffat. Moffat was the attorney who had been Henry Snow's friend many years before in New York, a former partner in the railroad, and had legally represented him during the first days the embezzlement story was leaking out. The Vermont Free Press Co. of Burlington had published the book in 1912.

Police were looking for Snow under his real name, not Clark. And Clark used a pseudonym, Sherwen N. Grayson, for his book, which was an anagram of Henry Sanger Snow.

Crockett's report continued:

Mr. Clark has been in the employ of the Caribbean Petroleum Company for several years in a fairly responsible position. He has also acted as agent or representative in Caracas of Mr. Addison McKay, the well-known American concessionaire and financial adventurer.

Mr. Clark is a small man of delicate physique and is almost deaf.

He is quite a clever man and has a good knowledge of Venezuelan political conditions and the psychology of the people. He is an intimate friend of Dr. Rafael Requena, the confidential go-between of General Gómez, the president (See dispatch No. 1258, dated September 7, 1923, subject Journey to the United States of Dr. Rafael Requena).

It is alleged that Mr. Clark is so closely associated with Dr. Requena that he repeats what is told him to the latter and has actually been the cause of more than one Venezuelan being imprisoned by General Gómez. It is even alleged that he is a paid spy for General Gómez.

The military attaché does not believe the last allegation to be true. It is his opinion that Mr. Clark tried to keep on good terms with General Gómez merely through motives of policy and not because of sympathy with his methods. The attitude of Mr. Clark nevertheless is one of subserviency and adulation to the dictator, and in this respect he is about on the same plane with the average native.

Several years ago, he was awarded the Venezuelan decoration of the *Orden del Liberador* for having presented General Gómez with an original letter, written by the *Liberador Bolívar*, which in some way had come into his hands.

Clark never stated directly that the gift of the letter resulted in the award. The award came more than a year after the gift to Gómez in 1919.

At one time, Mr. Clark was not on good terms with the dictator and wrote several semi-humorous articles regarding his rule for American publications, which however were never published. He was a warm friend of General Juan Pablo Peñaloza before the latter fell in disgrace with the dictator, and the escape of Peñaloza from Venezuela is said to have been due to Mr. Clark's assistance.

McGoodwin's dispatches to the State Department included details of Peñaloza's escape, which he had written immediately after it had occurred in 1914.

Well after the event, McGoodwin was no longer working for the government and was working in Caracas. He could have felt comfortable revealing Clark's role in the escape.

The military attaché is of the opinion that Mr. Clark, in the performance of his duties as press representative, is governed more by motives of expediency than by the wish to give truthful expression to facts and existing conditions.

Along with the report, Crockett enclosed a question-and-answer form from MID that he had filled out. Crockett again acknowledged Clark's language and writing skills. He also acknowledged Clark's political acumen, but he said that his general reputation was "doubtful, although some Americans speak highly of him."

He wrote that Clark was "probably not" discreet or trustworthy, and he answered yes when the form inquired about "any shady gossip?"

He complained again of what he called Clark's propaganda in favor of Gómez, and he mentioned Clark's almost constant access to Requena.

Crockett's personal relations with Clark, he wrote, were friendly, but he remained guarded about Clark because he didn't trust him.

He also noted that the Associated Press representative was paid about twenty dollars a month.

Crocket made this report on Clark in response to instructions from the War Department. In 1921, the War Department required all military attachés to routinely report on all American newspapermen in their areas. The department hoped to be better able to evaluate the stories of reporters. They suggested that the information that the reporters provided would be valuable in helping the department build up the Military Intelligence Reserve Corps.

If Crockett intended to pursue the rumors about Clark, he had no opportunity. Within four months, Crockett's personal drama was playing out in Venezuela.

Under fierce scrutiny in 1924, the major was recalled to the United States in July.

Early in the year, the Venezuelan government had threatened a Venezuelan named Dr. López with imprisonment if he didn't produce his father, who was suspected of being involved in a plot to overthrow Gómez. López was allowed only four days to produce his father.

He took residence in Crockett's house for safety, and he persuaded the major to help him escape from the country.

When the State Department learned of Crockett's role in the escape, they informed him that they would be replacing him in a matter of weeks.

Before Crockett left the country, the secretary of state warned the legation that his actions had violated the US policy of "abstinence from participation in the internal political affairs of the nation in which they are stationed."

The State Department felt that Crockett's actions weren't warranted, and they warned the legation members against such activities.

The department's attention to Crockett diverted its focus away from Clark. The military report that the attaché had written about Clark was routinely filed away without any action.

Clark at no time gave any indication that he was concerned about being found out at this point, taking no steps as he did to protect himself during the war when he realized that he was considered suspicious.

20

A DEATH IN THE FAMILY

In July of 1925, Snow's first-born daughter Marion died after a two-year battle with sarcoma of the ileum.

She was thirty-eight years old.

What had once seemed like a perfect life had gone terribly askew.

She had been living in Germantown with her husband, Philip Stoever; her daughter, Hope; her mother; and her nurse. They lived in a house on West Penn Street that her mother had purchased in 1912 after the family had returned from Europe.

Marion had enjoyed a prosperous and glamorous early life growing up into the privileged household in Brooklyn Heights. Her grand coming-out party was detailed in the society sections of the newspapers. Her vibrant life, however, had dimmed long before her illness. Her father's crime and disappearance had devastated the family's social standing, and family finances no longer allowed for extravagant parties. The notables among their dinner guests had dried up as soon as the crimes became public knowledge.

She'd accompanied the family to Europe in 1909, helping her mother get settled with her two younger sisters and brother. In

December of 1910, however, she returned to New York to stay with relatives. When Anna decided to return to the United States in 1912, Marion rejoined her family to assist Anna during the trip home.

Anna had been born in Philadelphia. It was natural for her to choose the nearby suburb to try to rebuild her life and the lives of her children.

Unlike Brooklyn Heights, not all residents of Germantown were familiar with her family's circumstances.

Marion had married Stoever in 1918. Anne, her sister, had married a Belgian man named Fernand Paternotte in 1916, and they lived with the family for a while in Germantown with their daughter, Annie.

With the sounds and activities of the two young girls around, it was a happier household than it would otherwise have been. Grandmother was more of a nurturer now with her societal career behind her. And Marion, who had been there to help raise her sisters, had been helping raise her sisters' daughters.

Marion's marriage to Stoever was fine at first, but it turned ugly as his alcoholism worsened. Sister Constance, who had also married by Marion's death, lived nearby in Germantown. She later recalled that Stoever had occasionally physically abused Marion. He had once pushed Marion to the ground, injuring her thigh.

Shortly after Marion's death, Philip remarried the nurse who had attended Marion during her illness.

The loss of Marion at an early age saddened her father. He was sixty-nine years old, and he'd already lost one son, David, many years before. Marion had been his favorite. She had been everyone's favorite. Snow was feeling guilty. The rest of the family had been around her when she died.

He hadn't seen his family since the February night in 1908 when he had stepped out the back door and vanished. Seventeen years had passed.

He hadn't ignored his family members, but he'd done little to help them since he had abandoned them.

He was aware that Anna's public life was gone, and she'd become reclusive, but he harbored hopes that the surviving children were well and perhaps prospering.

In Snow's absence, his family had weathered more turbulence and loss than most families.

He'd insisted for several years on receiving weekly letters from his children, even though Constance was the only one who actually tried to meet that standard. And she only did so because she wrongly blamed herself for his disappearance.

The exchange of letters kept Snow in relatively frequent contact with his children. He hoped that a visit could reassure them.

From an early age, Constance's life had been the most difficult. She'd been hurt the most by his disappearance.

She'd already been badly scarred by a rowboat tragedy that had killed Hulda Nelson, her governess, in 1905. She was three years old at the time of the accident.

The boat had tipped over, spilling Constance, the family laundress, and Hulda into the waters of Lake George, New York, where the family was vacationing.

From the dockside, the family's cook threw a rope into the water. He saved the laundress but Constance's beloved Hulda drowned.

Railroad magnate George Foster Peabody and his brother Charles were nearby in their launch and they heard the shrieking. They pulled Constance from the water.

She wrote of the tragedy much later, describing Peabody holding her upside down by her ankles to let the water run out of her.

Constance wrote that she felt responsible throughout her life for the accident. Constance had persuaded Hulda to ignore Father's rule not to play in the rowboats.

Constance became a somewhat contemplative and troubled child. She went through therapy for many years as an adult. She blamed herself for Hulda's death, and she came to conclude over several childhood years that the accident had somehow driven away her father.

She became conscious when she was young that the family was no longer highly regarded socially. Their loss of income had forced a significant reduction in their lifestyle. In her writings, she noted that she was no debutante. Unlike Marion, Constance had no coming-out party. As an adult, she wrote that she believed that her experiences had toughened her and prepared her for difficult times she had faced.

The Snows had not intended to have Constance. The Snow's second child was a beautiful son named David. After David died at three and a half years of age of meningitis in 1891, the Snows attempted to bear another male child. Edward Leslie arrived in 1892. Since Leslie looked average and was somewhat frail as a child, the Snows tried again. Two years later came Anne.

Still, Snow wanted another son. He had even decided to name his future son Henry. Instead, Constance came in 1902. Anna was forty-seven years old at the time. Anna decided that she had given birth to enough children.

The family had been forced to move to lesser quarters after Snow disappeared, and this left Constance feeling depressed. She found the new house dark and uninviting. Then a confrontation with some boys in the neighborhood led to a fistfight.

Soon afterward, someone claiming to be the Black Hand attempted to extort money from the family by threatening to kidnap Constance. This convinced Anna to flee with the family to Europe in 1909.

In 1919, Constance was hospitalized for thirty-seven weeks. Thirteen doctors agreed on a diagnosis of a heart problem, but they couldn't cure it. She was seventeen years old at the time. Feeling bored and frustrated, the girl rebelled, occasionally sneaking away when hospital personnel allowed her outside to sit in the sun.

She repeatedly demanded to be released. Anna eventually relented and took Constance on a trip to Europe for thirteen months in 1920 and 1921. Constance later viewed the trip as part of her rehabilitation.

Leslie's life had taken a somewhat different path. He mostly drifted away from the family. He'd traveled to Europe in 1909 with his family, but he returned to the United States in January 1911 for schooling. He was eighteen years old at the time, and he began studying engineering at Stevens Institute of Technology in Hoboken, New Jersey. After graduating, he remained in Hoboken. He did not want to be a financial burden to the family, and he was not yet equipped to provide much support for them.

He rented a room in the city and lived there until 1920, when he joined the United States Navy as a second-class engineer who was attached to the New York class battleship USS *Texas*.

When he was young, he'd suffered from rickets and a condition that prevented the full expansion of his chest. His health conditions improved, however. By the time he was in college, he was competing at tennis.

While Anna felt poorly treated by her husband, she'd continued to protect his identity. She allowed him access to their children and grandchildren during the visit.

Father landed in Brooklyn on Christmas Eve of 1925, and he took a train to Philadelphia to call at the home in Germantown. He stayed at a nearby hotel and visited the house on West Penn Street every day.

As always, he dressed in a wool suit, a high collar shirt, and a tie for these visits. He intended to give the family the impression that he was an accomplished man who had built a new life.

He focused his conversation on their time apart, questioning them about their experiences.

He dealt with his crime, his disappearance, and the abandonment by writing four detailed volumes about his life which ignored them. He turned over the volumes to his children years later. He made no apologies.

One journal, a biography of his life, ended before the revelation of his crime.

After he arrived in Caracas, he started a journal about his experiences in Venezuela. He recounted much of what had occurred to him during his lost years. He recounted how he'd gotten along, what he'd become, the people he'd met, and the adventures he'd experienced.

His conversations during his visits with the family mirrored the same memories that he would later write about.

He was comfortable discussing the people he'd met along the way, as he was always seeking to impress his family by talking about the important positions of the people he knew. He would talk about their trust and reliance on him.

He took special pleasure in describing various pitfalls he'd avoided with his ingenuity. These were the only times he made any references about his absence to his children, even though these references were even more subtle than those in his love poems to

Anna. He would describe his occasional need to obtain or possess a passport when traveling.

The family was shocked when Stoever had married Marion's caretaker. He had done so very quickly. She had been in their home for so long, and this situation worsened Philip's already shaky reputation with them. The couple moved but they continued to live nearby in Germantown, irking the siblings when they ran across them.

The unsettling nature of Stoever's actions, however, went unmentioned in Snow's later recounting of his visit.

> During the years of my absence, I had acquired three sons-in-law, none of whom I had the pleasure of knowing, so that I was extremely glad to have the opportunity to remedy that deficiency.
>
> It was very sad that dear Marion, who had died in the preceding July, was not with us, but Leslie, Anne, and Constance, I found well and happy, as also was dear Mother.

After going to Germantown, Snow took a train to Stamford, Connecticut, where Anne, Fernand, and little Annie had moved the year before. He stayed for a week and then sailed from Brooklyn to La Guaira in late January of 1926.

In his later recollections, Snow referred to another situation in which he had to be deceptive when he returned to Venezuela.

> I have omitted to note an amusing circumstance in connection with my New York visit. Before leaving, my associates reminded me that now passports

were absolutely necessary, both for entering New York and for returning to Venezuela.

I had no passport, but I felt sure that I could overcome the difficulty.

On arriving at New York, my passport was called for by the port authorities; I told them I had none, but that I could show them my commission as American vice consul at La Guaira, if they desired.

Good enough, responded the officer, and he did not require me to produce it.

On applying at the steamship office for my return passage, the agent told me that he could not sell me a ticket without seeing my passport, that this was absolutely required by Venezuelan law, if I wished to land at La Guaira.

"Do you require a passport for passage to Curacao," I inquired?

"No," he replied. "The Dutch do not require that."

"All right," I answered. "Give me a ticket for Curacao, and I'll have no difficulty in landing at La Guaira, where I know all the officials!" The Curacao passage was but five dollars more than to La Guaira. On reaching that port, I told my friend, the boarding officer, that I had taken passage for Curacao, but that I now found it unnecessary to go there.

"Muy bien," said he, and at once listed my name with the La Guaira passengers, no questions asked.

21

SOMETHING OLD, SOMETHING NEW

Anna Laconte Brooks Snow died on August 3, 1932 at seventy-seven years of age. She died in her home at 3216 Penn Street in Germantown.

The cause of her death was listed as diabetes and senility. At the time of her death, she was in the care of her son, Edward Leslie, with whom she shared the home. Leslie, who spent periods of his life away from Anna and the girls, had been working as an engineering foreman at the gas company. He and his mother had just returned from a trip to pick up ice cream.

Anna's obituary noted that she was the daughter of David Brooks, the inventor. It stated that she and her husband, Henry Sanger Snow, had lived in Brooklyn, where he had been a "well-known figure in civic and business affairs and for four years was president of Polytechnic Institute."

There was no mention of Snow's crime or his disappearance many years before. No survivors were listed. It didn't mention Anna's earlier friendship with Andrew Carnegie or his generosity to her.

Snow's grandchildren recalled a visit to Germantown by a man who was introduced to them as "Mr. Clark." They weren't told that he was their grandfather. They believe that this man had visited them sometime after Anna's funeral.

In his writings, Clark didn't mention the death of the woman he had been married to for forty-seven years. He had written poems to her about his love, and he had always referred to her as Dear Mother, but he didn't mention any more of this in his writings left for his children. Nor did he mention seeing her for the last time during a trip back to the United States the year before her death.

On September 22, 1932, seven weeks after Anna's death, Clark married a Venezuelan woman with whom he'd been living and with whom he'd had a son in 1923. The couple traveled to Puerto España, Trinidad, for the wedding.

Among those sending notes of congratulations was General Gómez. Clark's new wife was named Carmen Luisa Caballero. She was many years younger than Clark. Their son was named José Miguel. He was nine years old at the time of their marriage. They had met when they were both residents of a *pensión*, or guesthouse, in Caracas.

At the time of Anna's death, the Snow children had not been told about Carmen or the boy.

There had been exchanges of holiday cards over the years between the Snow children and their father. Everyone indicated warm feelings. Philip, Marion, Fernand, Anne, Leslie, and Constance had signed one letter that began, "To my father at Christmas."

Clark informed his children of his new wife and son shortly after Anna's death. While the others appeared to accept it well, a great angst arose in one son-in-law. He later reviled Clark in letters that he sent to him, berating his father-in-law with rants about his "new interests" and Clark's decision to leave his estate in Venezuela to Carmen and their son.

Fernand had been struggling with the cost of his wife's health problems for two years. He'd grown angry with what he felt was Clark's lack of support.

In the middle of January 1934, Fernand wrote to Clark in Caracas to inform him more fully of Anne's troubled health. He traced her condition to the death of her mother, which he said had caused her to suffer a nervous breakdown. He also referred to a previous letter he'd written to Clark. He had demanded that the estate be left to Clark's children in the United States.

He told Clark that he'd withheld the severity of Anne's illnesses from him because he had felt that sharing it wouldn't help her. He felt now, however, that he had to inform him "in justice to her."

Angered and bitter, Fernand revealed in his one-page, typed, and single-spaced letter that Anne had taken to her bed for two months after her mother's death. Afterward, she had rallied somewhat. However, Fernand said, a letter from Clark then arrived, and its message had sent Anne into immediate relapse.

> In that period [of recovery] came your letter with all that it implied, a ghastly revelation of disloyalty in the face of years of loyalty on the part of those you have left burdened and a flat declaration that you had decided to disinherit your daughters to the benefit of others. The shock of these revelations was a telling one. Anne suffered a relapse. In a considerably weakened condition, she contracted sciatica of a most acute type.

Fernand charged that Clark's letters, which made reference to Clark's wife and child and included photographs of the child, had "undermined" Anne's morale. He vowed that any future letters mentioning Carmen or the boy would be destroyed before Anne could see them.

He added, "I do not want any such things as the pamphlets, magazines, and others you are sending her to reach her. Such things have been and will be disposed of. Remember, you cannot atone for such wrongs by the offering of trifles."

It was clear that although he was aware of it, Fernand was not referring to Snow's desertion of his first family, but rather his recent decision to leave his estate to his family in Caracas. At the time, Fernand was fixated on the estate question.

Fernand explained his inability to care properly for her and his having to take her to Brussels so that his family could help care for her. While the ship crossed the ocean, she developed pneumonia.

From the time of her arrival there, in May of last year, until now, all that could be done for her has been undertaken. Seven doctors have been consulted, including the best talent we could find in Belgium, England, and Germany, and every remedy has been tried to cure the result of the sciatica, an acute curvature of the spine and a twisted body, which has made her an invalid.

My father and mother have contributed all they could and my brother has paid over one thousand dollars of bills. These efforts have proven fruitless, and I am now faced with the necessity of taking her as soon as possible to a warm climate in the hope that permanent heat and sunshine may help a condition where the cure is in doubt. To do this, I must sacrifice my position and we shall be leaving as soon as her condition permits.

> At your death, it will be your duty to leave to each
> of your children the maximum possible protection,
> regardless of preference for new interests.

He concluded the letter by telling Clark not to bother responding.

But Clark did respond. On February 26, 1934, he sent a letter to his son Leslie and daughter Constance, instructing them to forward it to Fernand. Clark wrote five full pages on yellow tablet paper. He said that he regretted the "serious burden" that Anne's illness had imposed on Fernand and his family. In the same paragraph, he suggested that Fernand had overstated Anne's health condition. His tone took on an officious attitude.

> I have duly received your letter of January 15, giving me, for the first time, full information respecting the nature, seriousness, and extent of Anne's illness.
>
> Not alone in justice to her, but to me, her father, that information should long ago have been given to me!
>
> I do not need to say that I am greatly concerned with regard to Anne, whose condition, I trust, has been possibly somewhat exaggerated by your anxiety.

Clark also confronted the inheritance question, explaining that his estate was small. He added that he'd sent his wife Anna money over the years to help pay for the family's upkeep.

In view of the concern which your present and prior letters disclose with respect to the ultimate disposition of the small property which I possess, now very considerably reduced by the events of the years of depression, I think it well to inform you respecting of some matters of which you are ignorant.

As the only surviving child of my parents, I was their sole heir and legatee. I drew both their wills. My father left his entire estate to my mother, and at her death, her property could descend to me.

His brother, Edward Leslie Snow, had died in 1893 at the age of thirty-five of chronic Bright's disease and asthma.

He told Fernand that he had changed his mother's will to more fully protect his family, saying that provision had full effect when his mother died in March 1908.

He also wrote, "Some ten or twelve years ago, an interest which I had entirely forgotten, belonging to me, was brought to my attention. It appeared that its value was some ten thousand dollars. That also, as with my mother's estate, was made over in its entirely to my wife. I believe she invested it in her house."

He truthfully described his working career from 1908 to 1918 as irregular. During this time period, he claimed, he was unable to meet his financial needs, and he had to rely on loans from friends for partial support. These loans went unpaid until he began work for the Caribbean Petroleum Company "at a small salary" in April 1918. Although his pay increased over time, he claimed that it was never substantial. Still, he wrote, he sent home one-third of his earnings to Anna.

All property which I possess, or have possessed, is the result of my savings while in the employ of the Caribbean Petroleum Company. Contrary to the impression which you appear to have formed, the sole purpose of that saving was for my care and support in my old age, when I should no longer be earning.

He underlined "for my care and support."

He decried Fernand's insinuations, taking exception to Fernand's call to disregard his "new interests," Carmen and the boy he called Chip. He scolded Fernand for lecturing him about his responsibilities to the Snow children.

I do not need your suggestion respecting any provision for my son and daughters of mature years. My affection for them is undimmed, and my desire to aid them insofar as I can is unquestioned! I am sure they believe this!

He also attacked Fernand for threatening to dispose of the letters that he had addressed to his daughter. He said, "I might suggest that the suppression or destruction of mail addressed to another is a rather serious offense and may involve criminal prosecution!"

He ended in a similar tone:

My regard for Anne and for you, through her affection for you has led me to write you more temperately than the character of your letter to me would inspire. I trust the enlightenment may serve to correct your mistaken ideas.

Yours very truly, C. N. C.

He addressed a separate letter to his son, Leslie. It was intended for both Leslie and Constance. Clark made reference to Fernand's letter, and he included a copy of his response, asking Leslie and Constance to forward it to Anne in their next communication with her. He typed his new letter on stationery bearing the name C. Norman Clark and the address Este 15, No. 46, Caracas.

> I am enclosing for you and Constance to read and forward the letter which I have just written to Fernand, in reply to one lately received from him. I wish you to enclose my letter to him without fail in the next letter you are sending Anne; or, if you know his present address, or if they are to come to the states shortly, you may either send the letter addressed directly to him or hold it until they arrive.

Constance shared Clark's letter and the one from Fernand to him with her husband, George Dallas. Dallas replied by making it clear that Fernand was alone in his feelings. Dallas said that all was forgiven within the family. He called Clark's response "a truly Christian and magnanimous letter."

He said that Clark had the love of all the Dallas family, including his own, "in this difficult and complex situation. What you have done has nothing to hurt anybody except spiritually, and I am sure we can better understand the temptations and weaknesses of each other. The purpose of this letter is to let you know you have one son-in-law who is proud of the past and appreciates you for what you were and are. Love, George."

In a letter that his son Leslie sent to Clark in March, Leslie showed that they remained close and in regular contact. He described Anne's condition, and he answered the questions that Clark had brought up in his recent letter. After thanking Clark for a check that he'd sent, Leslie added that it "will be a big help at this time, for as I wrote you I had drained the old bank account in very good style."

Leslie thanked him for sending Fernand's letter and for his response.

Of Anne, he wrote, she "has really been very ill, it is easy to see that! Neither Constance nor I were given a clear concept of the nature of her illness until after they arrived here. It seems she has had a somewhat rare disease of germ origin inflaming the nerves. Such a disease has to run its course in the same manner as typhoid, etc. She is quite deformed now, but not so badly as she was a few months ago. Constance received a jolt when she saw Anne."

He continued, "I believe Anne will eventually recover and suffer no permanent defect, or rather deformation. I was particularly glad to note that as far as I could discern, she appeared to be in a good mental state of mind. Both Constance and I thought she seemed more like her old self than we had seen for a number of years. She seems cheerful and pretty full of fun. I do not know what Fernand is going to do in the way of business. Anne's illness has been expensive. I do not think that Fernand exaggerated Anne's illness. I was as much in the dark as you were. So was Constance."

Leslie also spoke of a present he'd sent to his father by parcel post. The gift was an ear trumpet, which Clark had requested.

Responding to Leslie, Clark this time recalled "dear Mother." He noted that it was the forty-ninth anniversary of their marriage.

"We were married at your grandfather Brooks' house, the central one of three white marble houses just above Twentieth Street, on Chestnut, No. 2008." Mother was the loveliest bride in the world!"

Referring to Chip's severe illness, Leslie concluded by expressing his hope that "the youngster" was progressing. He expressed his distress that the recovery was slow. Leslie signed the typed letter, "With best love, devotedly."

In May, Clark wrote again. He asked more about Anne and whether she was able to write. He said that he had not received a letter from her since August 31, 1933, which was nine months before, from Brussels. Clark asked Leslie if Fernand had "poisoned her mind about Father!"

Robert Brandt

Henry Sanger Snow and Anna
Brooks Snow on their honeymoon in
1886 in Pittsfield, MA.

The Snows take a vacation in 1907
to retrace the route Henry and
Anna took on their honeymoon.
From left, Constance, Henry,
Anna, Edward Leslie, Marion,
and Anne.

"Father" holds Marion and David,
the first two children. David
died of meningitis at 3 1/3 years
of age.

The Snow children: Edward Leslie,
Marion, and Anne, about eight
years before their father vanished.
Constance was not yet born
when the photograph was taken.

Marion, the Snow's oldest and most
polished child, as a young adult.
It was she who led police through
the house to show them her father
wasn't there. At the time her
mother was under the care of
a doctor.

Clark, right, with Dr. William
Stewart, the U.S. Public Health
Surgeon and a frequent
coconspirator in Clark's
many intrigues. They are at the
U.S. consulate in La Guaira
when Clark was serving as vice
and deputy consul in 1914.

The Venezuelan Club in Caracas,
where Clark was one of several
North American members. He
met there frequently with
Venezuelan officials.

Like an adopted son, Rudolf
Dolge was revered in Venezuela.
Here he is being honored for
fifty years in Venezuela. He is
seventh from the left in the
front row, holding cane.

Mrs. Dolge on horseback in
Caracas. Clark lived with
the Dolges before the
United States entered
World War 1. After the U.S.
entry, he covertly accused
Dolge of disloyalty to protect
his own reputation.

General Juan Pablo Peñaloza,
whose escape from Venezuela
was engineered by Chameleon.

The Gran Hotel Klindt, Clark's
first home in Caracas, in the
age before cars came to
Venezuela.

The hotel's dining room where the U.S. colony met as dictator General
Cipriano Castro prepared to flee the country in 1908. Note the mirrors in
the dining room and room entrances on the second floor where Clark lived.

Captain Robert Kemp Wright,
chief of US intelligence
in Venezuela and Clark's
roommate during World War 1.

Little Chip, in photograph
taken by his father, at the
foot of the Carabobo
Monument, El Paraiso,
Caracas.

The author interviews
Dr. Manuel Caballero,
left, about his memories
of his uncle, C. N. Clark,
at the Hotel Avila, Caracas,
in October 2006.

Gómez, center, entertains
aboard the steamer Tacariqua
on Lake Valencia near his
estate at Maracay. To his right
is US Minister Preston
McGoodwin in the straw
hat. At far left is Don
Juancho, the dictator's
brother.

The gang that broke the British oil monopoly in
Venezuela. From left, Dr. Requena, personal
secretary and liaison to Gen. Gómez, Mrs.
Addison McKay, Fred Kay of Standard Oil, Mrs.
Requena, Mike Correa, Standard Oil, and Addison
McKay, Clark's roommate and host of the Sunday
Night Dinners in the early 1920s.

Clark, upper left, was
always in attendance at
the Sunday Night Dinners.

CPC's team in Caracas. Doyle,
center, front row, wearing his
ever present bowtie, and
Clark, third from left in back
row, wearing his ever present
standing high collar.

Clark at work as
sales manager at CPC
headquarters in Caracas.

The dictator, center, meets
with Dr. Requena, left, and Gen.
Juan Crisótomo Gómez, the
dictator's brother, at the
Maracay estate. Below,
with his brother, left, and
Provisional President
Márquez Bustillos. Clark
took both photographs.

In later years, Clark
owned a car in Caracas.
Caricatures in the local
press named it "The Red
Devil." Clark was depicted
with the top down and a
cigarette and holder
dangling from his mouth.

Clark, right, rests on
the grounds of Stanswood
House in Fawley, England,
home of Sir Henry and Hettie
Beaumont during visit in 1929.
With the Beaumonts in
photo at left is Frederic
D. Harford, who preceded
Beaumont as British minister
to Venezuela.

Guides led author, center,
to railroad trestle over
huge ravine between
Caracas and the shore.
Old railroad ties can be
seen jutting out from what
is now used as pedestrian
bridge. Standing next to
author is Amador Clark,
left, a Venezuelan television
producer, and Hector Perez
Marchelli, a writer, editor,
and researcher in Caracas.
This was part of the route
Peñaloza traversed by
handcar during his
escape from Venezuela.

22

THE FINAL CHAPTER

T he boy had lived at home confined to a hospital bed for most of his later years. As he'd aged, his condition had worsened and he became unable to move or speak. His parents had to watch over him constantly. They would move his head from side to side every waking hour. They tried to comfort him when the seizures came.

The boy was named Jose Miguel Clark, although his father always called him Chip.

Although his parents lovingly misinterpreted vague signs or illusory signals of progress occasionally, Chip never had any respite from his disease. His parents had once hoped that he could play outdoors again. Clark had spoken of this in letters to the Snow children back home. Clark had initially expressed his hope of moving out of the city and "up the hill" so that he could improve Chip's surroundings. Chip got to move to *Sabana Grande*, but his condition never improved enough for him to play outside again.

After Anna died and Clark had informed the Snow children about his second family, Clark had begun to frequently mention the boy's health in his letters to his other children. Nowhere in the letters that remain did Clark indicate the hopelessness of the boy's condition. He always implied that he had hope for the boy's improvement.

His love for and concern about Chip were obvious in the letters. He felt a strong bond for Chip that only a parent could feel. He doted over the boy.

One day, a painful molar forced Clark to call a dentist to come to the house to remove his son's tooth. The removal caused the boy great pain. Clark stood in the corner of the room. He was overcome with emotion, cringing at his son's suffering.

Family life became difficult for the Clarks. It centered on caring for Chip in the house, which Clark called Mi Retiro. The house was five kilometers from downtown Caracas. It was the first of several enclaves to spring up eastward, and it was connected to the city by the Ferrocarril Central railway. In that small house, Clark lived with Chip, Carmen, the shepherd dog Moritz, and the cat they called Kitty.

Four steps led up from the front yard to the veranda and the front door. Inside, the living room had rattan furniture.

There was no guest room, and when Carmen's family visited from Maracaibo in northwestern Venezuela, they had to go to a pensión downtown.

Carmen's brother Francisco and his son Manuel occasionally traveled from Maracaibo to see Carmen. Manuel was scared of the dog. Aunt Carmen was aware of his fear, and she always restrained it with a leash when he was visiting.

Manuel recalled seeing the gringos drinking bourbon during one trip. He referred to Doyle and Clark.

Clark wrote with seeming sadness about his situation with his second family and what they meant to him. He wrote about how much he had to rely on them. Referring to what would have been his forty-ninth wedding anniversary with Anna, he wrote:

I spent the anniversary quietly and happily, here with my little family. You cannot imagine, Leslie, what it is to me to have the companionship, care, and affection of Carmen, and Chip! I am now practically stone deaf; cannot hear a person speak who is sitting beside me and cannot hear anything without my trumpet, and imperfectly even with that.

For all business with people coming to the house, I have to rely on Carmen for talking and negotiating, and if people wish to communicate with me satisfactorily they must write it out and hand it to me.

You may imagine what my situation would be, were I alone here!

In 1940, Francisco and Manuel visited. Clark's hearing had further declined. Manuel recalled the Caballero family sitting in the kitchen and talking. Clark walked by, stopping in the doorway to exclaim, "Don't think that I am stupid. I just can't hear."

Manuel and his father were there because Chip had died.

"I got his clothes," recalled Caballero, who was twelve years old at the time of Chip's death.

The clothes fit. Although he was seventeen years old when he died, the boy was small. He had spent so much time, a lifetime it seemed, confined to a bed.

Chip's funeral was at Avenida de La Linea 61, Sabana Grande on December 9, 1940. Carmen's brothers attended, as did several of Clark's former colleagues from CPC. Leon Booker, William Phelps, and Harry Gibson were also there.

So much was behind him now. He was eighty-four years old. Gone were his parents, his brother Edward Leslie, his wife Anna, his sons David and Chip, and his daughter Marion. There was no more drinking bourbon with Doyle. He was gone. His friend Dr. Stewart was gone. His favorite chess opponent, General Peñaloza, was gone. Gómez had been gone five years.

Behind him was a world of lavish dinners at 270 Henry Street, daring escapes, friendships with ministers, Caracas evenings at the men's clubs, and games of chess.

Caring for Chip had dominated his life at home. With Chip gone, Clark's world centered on Carmen, the slightly chubby, curly headed woman who had borne him a child and kept his house at *Sabana Grande.*

EPILOGUE

Such, in synthesis, is the story of
my life during the many years which I have
spent in Venezuela. I have endeavored to
recall the salient incidents and
experiences for your information and
entertainment, giving some account of my
various occupations, of my friendships, and
something of the amusing or unusual events
which may serve to enlighten my story.

> To my Children, Leslie, Anne,
> and Constance
> Father, Caracas, October 14, 1937

Henry Sanger Snow (*Alias Cyrus Norman Clark, C. N. Clark, C. Norman Clark, Norman C. Clark, Dr. Norman Clark, Grayson N. Sherwen*).

Snow died in Caracas in 1944 at eighty-seven years of age. Survivors included his wife, Carmen Lucia Caballero de Clark, and his three children, Leslie, Anne, and Constance Snow. His death was caused by renal and cerebral arterial sclerosis on March 24 at 3:00 p.m. at his home, El Recreo. He was buried at Cementerio del Municipio Liberador on March 25.

Among the fifty-three attendees at his funeral were Leon Booker, William Phelps, Juan Bautista Bance, B. Th. W. Van Hasselt, Clare Taylor, Rudolf Dolge, Arthur Bonal, Henry E. Linam, Dr. Rafael Max Valladares, Stewart E. McMillan, and Pablo Peñaloza.

Clark had worked at CPC until he was seventy-five years old. He retired in 1931.

As late as 1941, Clark was still "on the job," stirring up the US military in Argentina when he called on an attaché at Buenos Aires as a correspondent for the *New York Herald Tribune.* He asked for a comment on an exclusive report he had from two agents of US airplane makers. The agents had stated that the Vickers Company of England had offered to deliver Fairey fighters to the Argentine government. The report went immediately to the US legation, which contacted Clark to express its concern about how the US public might react if it were published.

He lived with Carmen for another three years until his death. After thirteen years of service, he received a pension from CPC of one hundred twenty-five dollars a month. The pension, "with the income from investments of my Provident Fund, has enabled me to live comfortably during these latter years." He explained the workings of the fund and how he had accumulated twenty-five thousand dollars through his salary withholdings and through the company matching his funds.

It is unclear when Snow last communicated with his son and his daughters in the United States, although his Venezuelan nephew in Caracas recalled seeing a letter in the Clark home that was addressed to his son Leslie around 1940.

Edward Cipriani

While Cipriani remained with the Consular Service until his death, his economic condition never noticeably improved. In 1921, he wrote to Mr. Hengstler again. This time, he wrote to lament his own failure to pass the consular examination.

This, he reported, was a "crushing blow to me and probably means the breakup of my family life."

He wrote that as yet he hadn't the courage to inform his wife. Being in poor health, she would likely experience a "complete nervous breakdown."

He spoke of a winter of suffering in Leeds, England, where he was then based. He pleaded with Hengstler to save his family from another such winter by assigning him to Trinidad, which he so fondly remembered.

A month later, he was reassigned to Glasgow, Scotland, where within four months the department was admonishing him for failing to meet personal financial obligations in Leeds and Glasgow. This had brought embarrassment to the service. He was still in Glasgow in 1925, pleading for a raise so that his children back in the United States might have Christmas dinner.

After becoming ill following lunch, he died in Glasgow on May 29, 1927. A nurse at a hospital informed his daughter that he was suffering from indigestion after overeating but was in no danger. He died in the hospital two days later and was buried in Glasgow. The official cause of his death was ruled as heart failure.

Carmen Lucia Caballero de Clark

Although she was thirty years younger than Clark, Carmen survived her husband by only one month. In that month, however, she changed Clark's will, just as he had done with his mother. Clark had left his Venezuelan estate to Carmen, but the will called for the property to go to his children in the United States when Carmen died. Carmen replaced that portion and left everything to her brothers. Included was the prized refrigerator, for which the family was thankful. Carmen had suffered seizures before she knew Clark. She was embarrassed about this, and she never spoke of them to him. In her final month, she had begun suffering them again.

C. N. Clark (The Real One)

Clark was a civic activist in New York who was known as the Father of the West Side. He was a director of Hamilton Bank of New York. He was a founding member of the Executive Committee, and he was later the president of the West Side Association. The group initiated the construction of Riverside Drive. After his death in 1909, associates commissioned a memorial in his honor by sculptor Henry Kirke Bush-Brown, which was imbedded in a natural rock outcropping near the Eighty Third Street entrance to Riverside Park. Henry Sanger Snow was named after Henry Sanger, his father's business partner. Henry Sanger's wife had a sister who was married to C. N. Clark.

Clarke and Kuhne

Pressured to explain how they had let Snow get away, District Attorney John F. Clarke and Captain August Kuhne stepped all over each other in the days following Snow's disappearance. Clarke claimed that it was he who had seen the severity of the allegations against Snow, and he had stepped forward to obtain the indictment. At the same time, Detective Kuhne claimed that he wasn't told that a felony indictment would be forthcoming until late on the Thursday on which Snow was last seen in New York.

Had he known earlier, Kuhne said, he would have had Snow watched more closely.

Rudolf Dolge

Dolge's notable contributions to Venezuela included his highly regarded library on Venezuela, which he left to the country for an agreed-upon price. He lived to complain that the Venezuelan government was reneging on its promise of payment. He died in Caracas in 1950, outliving all of the American colleagues he'd welcomed to Caracas during the "early days." He first arrived there in 1897. He was buried with his father, his wife, and his son in the Dolge family cemetery in Dolgeville, Herkimer County, New York.

William T. S. Doyle

Doyle died in Caracas on January 1, 1940, two weeks after retiring from Shell. The cause of his death was cirrhosis of the liver. Clark wrote Doyle's obituary for the newspaper *Crítica*. Like Clark, Doyle was buried in Caracas.

He and Clark maintained contact until his death. It was in 2006 when Carmen's nephew Manuel remarked he would never forget seeing the "gringos" drinking whiskey at the Clark house.

In one letter to his son Leslie, Clark related, "By great good fortune, I found just two bottles of bourbon left in stock in one of our supply houses, the last they had, for no one here drinks anything but Scotch!"

After meeting in 1908 at the Hotel Klindt, Doyle and Clark knew each other for thirty-two years. Doyle had corresponded with him through 1912, when Clark sought project concessions from Venezuela. Doyle worked with him at the oil company and nursed him through two illnesses and a surgery.

Like Clark, Doyle's first wife died. He also took a younger Venezuelan bride, and he had two children with her.

John Peter Jens Duhn (Alias John Paul Jones Duhn)

After World War I, Duhn explained his return to the United States for his associates at the Office of Naval Intelligence.

"After nursing a friendship and intimacy with Carl Fensohn, German consul on this island [Curacao], obtained the German Admiral's Code Book with key and instructions for use, which were left in his charge by the German Imperial Navy captain of the *Karleruhe*, the auxiliary cruiser sunk near St. Thomas Island by posing as a confidence man of the German minister in Caracas, Mr. von Prollius."

"After an unsuccessful attempt of two other German agents [Spaniards] to take these things away from me, Captain Wright cabled for protection to Panama, and the United States Coast Guard cutter *Ithaska* took me from San Juan, Puerto Rico, to Key West, Florida, where Rear Admiral Anderson received and dispatched me for Washington. I arrived here again on January 2, 1918."

Duhn was at the time engaged to marry the daughter of the former German consul at Charleston, South Carolina.

After the war, Duhn's life dulled considerably. While working at a disinfectant company in Washington, he applied for a job as consul with the State Department. He was rejected. The director of the Justice Department's Bureau of Investigation, William J. Burns, pleaded with MID to find a suitable position for Duhn in 1924.

Burns said, "He is one of the unfortunates whose public service is not advertised during the war. He was one of the international operatives working for several departments of the government, including our own. The records of the Navy Department will show that he was the only foreign agent of the United States who captured a secret German code, and I am given to understand that five submarines are to his credit."

Duhn didn't marry the former German consul's daughter. In 1930, he was living in Wheaton, Maryland. He worked as a telephone salesman. He eventually moved to Silver Spring, Maryland. He worked in Washington, DC, at Elixo Plant Food Company, Inc., which was owned by his wife, Cora Mae Duhn.

Charles Freeman

The intelligence leaks from the American legation to the German legation in Caracas in 1917 and 1918 grated on Captain Wright. He blamed the leaks on Freeman and his close relationship with McGoodwin during the war years.

In 1922, Venezuelan revolutionary leaders gave up on US help and approached Freeman in the hope that he would appeal to the British minister to gain that country's help in overthrowing Gómez. The US military attaché who reported this, however, said that he had spoken to the British minister, who "expressed the opinion to me the other day that the continuation of control by Gómez would be the best thing for the Venezuelans and everyone else concerned."

For several years during the 1920s, the Gómez regime harassed Freeman. It sought to oust him from the country. The US State Department interceded on behalf of Freeman, and they eventually resolved the matter. In 1927, Freeman visited Gómez at Maracay for several days, and he returned to Caracas "again on friendly terms with President Gómez."

Juan Vicente Gómez

The dictator's seizure of Venezuelan assets never abated while he lived. The *Gaceta Oficial* was a government publication of laws, decrees, appointments, awards, and recognitions. In 1931, this publication reported an exchange of property between Gómez and the government.

Gómez traded some land at Maracay to the government for properties in the State of Miranda. These properties included the electric light plant, a hydroelectric plant at Las Delicias, a cattle-slaughtering plant at Maracay, the municipal theater at Maracay, and other hydroelectric plants at Maracay. The publication placed the value for each property in the exchange at 7,014,720 bolivars.

George Summerlin, the US minister at the time, said that most people would have called these trades "plain steals." However, since Gómez considered all of Venezuela his personal property, it had to be viewed in a different light.

Major Crockett understood well the cleverness of Gómez's reign, and he was articulate in explaining it.

His system is unique and challenges the admiration even of the Anglo-Saxon residents. It functions so smoothly that it would be impossible to get legal proof before any tribunal on earth that General Gómez is not the constitutional president of Venezuela and likewise that all his acts are not by virtue of the constitution and laws of the country.

But to the observer who understands the situation, there are two motives to every act of the government, national or local. First, the ostensible motive, usually having to do with the public welfare, and secondly, the actual and hidden motive, almost invariably one of graft which, if the sums involved are of sufficient importance, extends up to the family of the dictator.

Explaining how Gómez amassed huge fortunes, Crockett explained the monopoly that the dictator held in cattle, and he also explained how Gómez enforced this monopoly.

Orders are given prohibiting the slaughter of uninspected cattle in Caracas, the ostensible motive clearly being to ensure that good meat be provided.
The hidden motive, however, is that Gómez holds the monopoly for providing cattle for slaughter and the inspectors would not pass the cattle of another person, even should anyone have the temerity to try to make a sale, an impossible contingency in view of the fear with which Gómez is regarded.

Clark acknowledged the worst about the dictator, but he found ways to overlook it.

That the general was a dictator; that he was moved by insatiable ambition; that he enormously enriched himself and his family at the expense of the nation; that he suppressed individual liberty and the freedom of the press absolutely; and that he was merciless with political adversaries and with all whom he knew or suspected of opposing his policies, none of this can be denied.
These were, nevertheless, conditions affecting only his own people, the Venezuelans. Toward the foreign residents within Venezuela, he was uniformly kindly and considerate. I came to know him well, early in my life in Caracas. After he came to know of my interest, through my connections with

the American press, to promote cordial relations between our two countries, he was unfailing in manifesting his friendship. On my frequent visits to Maracay, his favorite residence, he always gave me most cordial welcome.

I once found him at Maracay seated on the grass, with his little grandson on his lap and surrounded by a group of laughing children. The general was fond of children, and well he might be! He had never married but was the happy progenitor of a numerous progeny. Dr. Requena, his intimate friend and later his private secretary, told me that on one occasion he had asked the general how many children he had.

Ochentiuno y pico, (eighty-one and a little more, meaning one on the way) replied the general.

Other accounts of children fathered by Gómez indicated that he had only slightly fewer children.

After twenty-seven years as the dictator of Venezuela, Gómez died in 1935.

Erich Hirschfeld

In July 1921, Hirschfeld was back in Berlin. This time, he was plotting with Venezuelan exiles to overthrow Gómez and install José Maria Ortega Martínez as the president of Venezuela.

When he didn't receive the amount of money he had expected from the exiles for his roles in the plot, he tipped off the Venezuelan minister at The Hague and US military agents in Berlin. The Dutch government seized a ship, the *Odin*, which was being outfitted with weapons in Antwerp, and the British

Admiralty seized a second vessel, the *Harrier*, at Swansea Dock, south Wales, and removed enough machinery to disable it.

Preston McGoodwin

In the *Oklahoma Almanac*, which was published by the Oklahoma Publishing Company, the "Important Events of the Year (1929) in Oklahoma" included the following listing for June 12: "Announced that Preston McGoodwin Jr., son of Preston McGoodwin Sr., former editor of the *Oklahoman*, later American minister to Venezuela and now a resident of that country, shortly to wed daughter of Juan Vicente Gómez, the president of Venezuela."

Cornelius Van H. Engert, the American chargé d'affaires in Caracas, wrote to the State Department in 1929 to report that McGoodwin wasn't "making much headway" in his efforts to get a contract with the Venezuelan government for Pan American Airlines, which McGoodwin represented at the time.

Engert attributed his lack of success to two things. He claimed that McGoodwin's many enemies were "working against him," and he suggested that McGoodwin might have been wary of pushing the government too hard because of other "irons in the fire," including his oil interests. He also said "his son is about to marry the daughter of the minister of finance." There is no evidence that either marriage ever took place.

In 1946, Westbrook Pegler took an interest in targets of the Dies Committee. In his column on January 17, he reported that a man named Sam Carp of Bridgeport, Connecticut, was again appearing before the committee—he had first done so in 1939—to explain the facts surrounding his attempt to purchase an American battleship for the Soviet Union.

Carp was born in Russia. He had been in the United States for decades, but his sister remained in Russia and married Vyacheslav Molotov, a Stalin underling who held various official positions in the government.

In previous testimony, Pegler noted, Carp had acknowledged making payments to two men to help him obtain the ship.

Pegler wrote, "Carp and others related that he had paid fifty-seven thousand dollars altogether to Scott Ferris and Preston McGoodwin, deserving Democrats of the New Deal, for public relations and contacts in Washington while he was trying to get the super-battleship for Russia, under the impression that he could buy a battleship as casually as he might buy a tomato."

In an earlier column, Pegler reported that Carp had paid McGoodwin twenty-five thousand dollars in two payments in 1937 and 1938. Not making progress, McGoodwin suggested that Carp hire an attorney. McGoodwin had introduced Carp to Ferris, who was then a member of the Democratic National Committee. Ferris reportedly knew Cordell Hull, who was then secretary of state, as well as President Roosevelt.

In 1929, the US vice consul at La Guaira wrote to Engert to say how troubled he was when Venezuelan and US residents had spoken openly about McGoodwin's alleged corruption. He asked Engert how he should respond to such claims. Engert told him that people were always seeking to harm the reputation of the United States, and he encouraged the vice consul to do all in his power "to put a stop to silly rumors." Engert's insinuations to the State Department implied he thought otherwise.

McGoodwin died in 1945 in Lynchburg, Virginia, after a short illness. A few years before, he had retired to Altavista, Virginia. He was buried at Green Hill Cemetery on Bedford Avenue, the street that had been his residence in Altavista. His small, flat headstone notes his service as minister to Venezuela. No other family members are buried near him.

Jean Curtice McGoodwin
Jean died on February 22, 1962, at the Kensington Gardens Nursing Home in Maryland. Her residence at the time was listed to be 2032 Belmont Road, NW Washington. She isn't buried with her husband. She is buried at Rock Creek Cemetery in Washington, D.C., a facility that serves, among others, American diplomatic and consular families. Those residing there include Alice Roosevelt Longworth.

Addison McKay
The man who broke the British oil monopoly in Venezuela eventually turned his attention to Canada. He was one of the first people to win an iron ore concession in Labrador in 1934. When he died in Montreal in 1949, he was the director of the Labrador Mining and Exploration Co. He was also the vice president and director of the Quebec Smelting and Refining, Ltd. and the president of Kaymack Investments Ltd. and McKay Exploration.

General Juan Pablo Peñaloza
Peñaloza conducted numerous raids across the Colombia border into Venezuela until Gómez's troops captured him in western Venezuela in May 1931. He was imprisoned at Puerto Cabello prison, and he died there on June 17, 1932.

Peñaloza's relatives called on Clark to contribute to his headstone. The Venezuelan friends of Peñaloza were hesitant to do so, fearing retribution from Gómez. After fleeing Venezuela in 1914, Peñaloza had spent the rest of his life in exile in Colombia, Curacao, and New York City, where he lived at the Plaza.

George Benjamin Pengelly

Pengelly, the first man Clark helped to escape from Venezuela, had more trouble with the law after returning to England. For twelve years, Pengelly looked after the financial affairs of an actress named Edith Marion Rosse and Arthur Maundy Gregory, a man who boarded at her home. When Rosse died in 1933, she left everything to Gregory. It was discovered that Gregory had handwritten the will in pencil. It was also discovered that Gregory was short of funds.

The will stood up and no charges were filed against Gregory. Pengelly was called to testify at the inquest.

The very next year, Pengelly was called to appear at Old Bailey on charges of blackmail. His victim was the patriarch of Jerusalem. According to the prosecution, on January 9, 1934, Pengelly had sent a letter to the patriarch threatening to publish, either in the press or in a book, "matters and things which he thought that gentleman would be willing to give him money to suppress."

At the trial, Pengelly defended himself. He hoped to draw sympathy with a description of his physical infirmities. He was convicted and drew a sentence of six months. He was convicted again in 1937 for converting fifty pounds in stock shares to his personal use, having sold shares in a Canadian silver venture. However, he wasn't in possession of these shares. He was sixty-two years old, and he drew a prison term of nine months.

The blackmailing of the patriarch wasn't a novel idea. Gregory had earlier been convicted on the same charges. At Gregory's trial, the prosecution had submitted checks that he'd sent to the patriarch as evidence of his scheme to purchase Knighthoods of the Holy Sepulcher from the patriarch, which he planned to bestow on others in exchange for money. In blackmailing the patriarch, Pengelly threatened to disclose these sales.

Thomas Voetter

Although Voetter's career in the Foreign Service would continue for years, his job performance never improved. After a second bruising report by Eberhardt in 1915, Voetter received a formal letter of instruction from the State Department. Voetter was then serving as consul in Antofagasta, Chile.

In January 1922, Voetter returned to Venezuela. He had been assigned to Caracas. In July 1924, a new posting took him to Curacao. He received poor ratings that year, as well as 1925 and 1926. His efficiency report in 1927 led to him being demoted two grades from Class VI to Class VIII. In a letter of reprimand, the department warned him that if he did not improve his "poor" rating, they might terminate him.

In his response, Voetter indicated that he intended to try to correct his numerous deficiencies. He apparently was unsuccessful. From his post in Curacao in 1929, Voetter wrote the department that "advancing years and impaired health [were] decreasing his capacity for the performance of his duties, and consulate staff is very much undermanned." He retired on June 30, 1933. His last posting was in Guaymas, Mexico.

Captain Robert Wright

Captain Robert Kemp Wright was based in London in 1919. He no longer chased spies, and he had mellowed once the war had ended. A letter to Clark in December informed that the Selection Board in Washington had promoted him to the rank of commander in the Fleet Reserve.

He included a copy of a letter to Mrs. Wright from their son's commanding officer during the war, noting the son's devotion to duty and his death on the battlefield. Wright recalled his son's playmates in Caracas. He mentioned Alfred Dolge and Jack Lunford.

Lunford was an Englishman who was born in Caracas and served with Canadian forces in the war. Wright noted that both of these men had died during the war as had his son Preston. Wright said that he felt that Dolge and Lunford should be honored just as those who fell on the "field of battle." He asked Clark to extend his heartfelt sympathy to their mothers.

Maracaibo Bar

The sandbar remained an obstacle to the entrance to Lake Maracaibo until June 2, 1956. A three-year dredging operation opened the lake to ocean-going vessels on June 2, 1956.

The *Kermia* of the Netherlands left for Europe with a cargo of one hundred fifteen thousand barrels of oil from Shell Company wells. The project cost fifty-six million dollars, and it involved five companies.

Four of the five construction companies were American. The three-phase project required the construction of an inner channel, a two-mile breakwater into the gulf to hold back the shifting sands, and an outer channel. Until that time, the shallow draft barges brought out the oil or the pipeline pumped it out.

Margarita Island

ONI eventually scoffed at the issue of Margarita serving as a fueling depot for enemy submarines. "The entire question under consideration is reported to me to have been investigated many times, and in Trinidad it is known as the *chestnut*," wrote H. Henneberger Jr., commander of US Naval Forces in the Canal Zone, to the director of the Office of Naval Intelligence in April of 1918.

Two months later, ONI reported to the British naval attaché in Washington that another search had been made. The officer determined that Margarita wasn't at all suitable for a submarine base. The waters were "too shallow and exposed." All was quiet on the island, the officer reported.

Oddly, Diego Guzmán Blanco, the son of the former president of Venezuela, walked into the US Embassy in Paris in June 1918 and told the ambassador, William Graves Sharp, that he believed that German submarines could replenish their fuel supplies at a small island off of the Venezuelan coast. His uncle, General Matos, had once fitted out a ship at Hamburg and sailed for Martinique, where the ship was equipped for war and continued under the Venezuelan flag.

"It made its supply base on a small island to windward of the chain of islands from Aves to Margarita; this island, of which he does not recall the name, is about one mile long and forty feet high and cannot be sighted at any considerable distance." It is possible, Sharp quoted Guzmán, that a "Venezuelan petrol company called the Felicidad sends petrol in coastwise vessels from Maracaibo either to La Hacha in Colombia, whence it is sent to the said island in vessels carrying the Colombian flag, but supplied with papers for ports on the Orinoco or else direct in Venezuela coast trade vessels under similar circumstances. He thinks that Mr. Norman Clark either American vice consul at La Guaira or clerk at the American Legation at Bogotá would be able to give information, or else proceed to Maracaibo to obtain information."

The Oilmen of Venezuela

Many people shared Clark's admiration for Doyle, but Americans would criticize him in later years when US actions that often seemed to support Gómez came under harsher evaluation. It was finally accepted in petroleum circles and by the US military that CPC had become a property of Royal Dutch Shell. US military interests criticized Doyle's complete dedication to the firm as bordering on anti-American.

The myth that the Caribbean Petroleum Company was a US company lived well beyond McGoodwin's tenure as minister in Venezuela. It was front-and-center again in 1929, when there was yet another challenge to the original concession.

After conducting an extensive investigation, the State Department's Office of the Solicitor pilloried McGoodwin again for his role in the earlier concession challenges.

"In spite of this data, which seemed to make it fairly clear that the Caribbean Petroleum Company was controlled by foreign capital, Mr. McGoodwin deemed it advisable to make somewhat urgent but 'informal representations' to the minister for Foreign Relations of Venezuela on behalf of the Caribbean Petroleum Company.

"It appears that as a result of McGoodwin's 'informal representations,' he was able to persuade the appropriate Venezuelan officials to have the suit to invalidate the company's concession heard on appeal by the High Court of Venezuela 'en banc' instead of by a single associate justice.

"It was apparently believed that a ruling by the entire court was advisable, presumably on the ground that it was more difficult 'to reach' several judges than one."

The report indicated that McGoodwin "was considerably influenced in the course he followed by Mr. W. T. S. Doyle, former chief counsel and afterward general manager of the company, and incidentally former chief of the Division of Latin American Affairs in the State Department."

After the death of Gómez in 1935, the new American minister in Caracas, Meredith Nicholson, couldn't avoid noticing the blame that was being aimed at the United States by ordinary citizens of Venezuela for the Gómez years. He wrote a harrowing summation of Gómez and his relations with the oilmen, several of whom had come from the US State Department, including Doyle, Proctor, and Stabler. In his "strictly confidential" dispatch to the State Department in 1936, Nicholson characterized them as "imperialists." He said that they deplored US foreign policy, especially in Latin America, and they voiced contempt for the new Venezuelan president and his tolerance and efforts at democracy.

In a series of reports to Washington over the summer, Nicholson referred to the "triumvirate" of Doyle, Leon Booker, and Stabler. He labeled them as dinosaurs and believers that "might, in the business sense, was right." They believed, he wrote, that US Marines should follow American investments around the globe.

He labeled Doyle "hard-boiled," and he said that Doyle dictated orders to the two others.

He found Booker to be intellectually inferior to the other two, and he said that Doyle and Booker derided Stabler "for his social and cultural pretensions."

He said that Stabler's "congenital snobbishness, his display of a monocle only when European visitors arrive, and his lonely devotion to polo in a community that looks upon a predilection for that sport as an advertisement of mental weakness have not contributed to his value in this capital as the representative of an important business."

The three men, Nicholson said, viewed the new and more tolerant regime as "inimical to the future of the oil companies established in Venezuela."

He quoted Stabler as remarking to an employee at the legation that he was "a reactionary, an imperialist of the old school who regarded the modern policy of nonintervention in the internal affairs of Latin American nations as nothing short of disastrous."

The "triumvirate" looked "askance" at the legation, according to Nicholson. It didn't share its information with the minister, he wrote. His assessment charged that it was "a notorious fact that under the Gómez regime the companies took advantage of the prevalent corruption to bribe their way to smooth sailing and that a substantial percentage of their profits went back into the country in the form of 'gifts' to key officials." The oilmen, he said, served as "grafting agents of the Gómez despotism."

That wasn't all. Nicholson wrote, "I consider it my duty to refer also to the reputed association of various foreigners with certain immoral practices, gross and shocking in the extreme, designed for the entertainment of government officials, which were common under the unprincipled and profligate rule of the late Venezuelan dictator.

However, as far as morality is concerned, it is no secret whatever that Mr. Booker is the father of a twelve-year-old illegitimate son, born of a Venezuelan mother, and that Mr. Doyle lived openly for many years in Caracas with a Spanish circus performer by whom he had two offspring and whom he eventually married after the death of his wife."

There seemed to be no length to which Doyle wouldn't go to protect Shell's oil domination in Venezuela. In 1925, there were rumblings of another concession challenge. This time, there was a challenge to Shell's Venezuelan Oil Concessions. These events propelled Doyle to explore a partnership with Gómez. This partnership would result in his company's control of all oil reserves in the country.

His scheme was simple. A company would be formed between Royal Dutch Shell and the National Petroleum Company of

Venezuela to take over control of all federal reserves as they were returned to the government at the end of concession contracts. Shell and the government would each hold 50 percent of the stock in the new company.

The US companies immediately appealed to the State Department for intervention. The new secretary had been in office for only one month. He instructed the minister to say to Gómez, "This government would view with concern any action which would tend to create a substantial monopoly to participate in future developments of the petroleum resources of Venezuela."

Two months later, the State Department was called on to counter rumors about a new player bidding for concessions. It was William F. Buckley and his Pantepec Oil Company. The rumors, which were attributed to Shell, charged that Buckley was a revolutionist in Mexico who "may have a similar purpose in Venezuela." As a result, he was in disfavor with the US government. The minister was instructed to approach the Venezuelan government, if necessary, to report that there were "no grounds" for the rumors.

Throughout the reign of Gómez, Doyle was viewed as a strong supporter of Gómez, but in 1936, after Gómez's death, the Venezuelan press published charges that Doyle had entered into a conspiracy in 1929 with General Vincencio Pérez Soto, who was then the president of the oil-rich state of Zulia. They planned to break the state away from Venezuela and declare an independent republic, and they intended to claim all of the revenues of the oil concessions there.

El Universal, the leading newspaper in Caracas, carried a full-page reprint of another publication, *Panorama*. This publication had run a reprint of an article from *Colombia Nacionalista*, which was where the story had originated. *El Universal* acknowledged that it couldn't guarantee the veracity of the article.

Doyle, the author of the article wrote, feared that the 1929 challenge to the British concessions could go against Shell. To protect the company, Doyle was reported to have prevailed on the US minister to deliver an ultimatum to Gómez, warning him not to allow the Royal Dutch Shell concessions to be ruled invalid. The story intimated that the pressure was financial in nature, but it offered no other details. When Gómez ordered the court to rule for Shell, the article claimed that Doyle backed away from the Pérez Soto conspiracy.

Gómez long feared that Zulia would become a breakaway state. He had reason to worry. In 1918, revolutionists approached the US consul at Maracaibo and asked him if the United States would recognize them and offer moral support if they took over control of the state.

NOTES

Henry Sanger Snow wrote of the events of his extraordinary life in four journals, which he presented to his three surviving children in the United States sometime after 1934.

He titled the chronicles *Biographical Memoranda, Recuerdos de Venezuela 1908-1933 C. Norman Clark, Venezuelan Reminiscences,* and *Varied Verses and Random Rhymes.*

He portrayed himself as a highly energetic, articulate, and observant man of taste. He was a product of his privileged childhood. Other of his descriptions and his actions cast him as a daring provocateur who was willing to go to risky extremes.

Nothing satisfactorily explains his crimes or his decision to run. His love poems to Anna make only vague suggestions of unwise decisions.

Written in his reserved style, Clark's accounts were mostly true except in two cases. In the case of Benjamin George Pengelly, the Briton who murdered his boss at the La Guaira port works, Clark portrayed an innocent man caught up in a corrupt government prosecution after an accidental death. In fact, Pengelly murdered his boss after being accused by him of a substantial embezzlement. No wonder Clark could not be truthful given his own background.

In the cases of Rudolf and Anita Dolge, Clark wrote of close friends for whom he cared. He wrote warmly of living with them and accepting their hospitality, which he found much preferable to other living options in Caracas. He gave no reason for not living with them during wartime and he never suggested or described how he used them as pawns with US military intelligence. Military records show clearly that he did.

Anna spoke little of Snow after he disappeared, and consequently his children were left to understand only what they could observe and assimilate. Only Marion was old enough to understand what had occurred.

Three grandchildren retained the four volumes and many family mementoes, but they can relate little else about their grandfather.

Anna told the children that Snow had simply gone crazy. She said, "I have been thrown on the ash heap."

The evidence against him was no doubt strong, but he had friends like Burnham Moffat and George Marshall Allen who could have been respectable character witnesses. Given Snow's civic activities, his positions at Brooklyn Polytechnic Institute, and the general high regard in which he had been held, an attorney could have presented a sympathetic defense, if not a conclusive one. Anna once blamed Snow's vanishing on "bad legal advice." There is no evidence that Snow consulted any attorney other than Moffat, or what Moffat advised him.

The week before Snow's indictment and disappearance, Moffat noted that he was not a criminal attorney. Would he advise Snow to run? There is some evidence that he was involved in misinforming police about one of the false escape scenarios.

Without much conviction, one grandson explained that Snow was one of three men in the same office where the embezzlement occurred. He claimed that they decided to draw straws to see who would take the blame. Snow, according to this explanation, drew the short straw.

This account probably emanated from a newspaper article' at the time that named a member of the staff who had received some company stock. The company quickly corrected the newspaper account that suggested wrongdoing, and it said that that employee was entitled to the stock.

Another theory is that Snow had been unable to keep up with Anna's expensive taste and lifestyle, and he simply overspent. This theory seems to be founded in conversations between Anna and her daughter, Constance.

Constance later wrote, "It is apparent to me that Mother felt horribly guilty. I think she felt that she had been too ambitious for us all and had in some way driven Father to embezzlement."

Snow's childhood offers no suggestion of what went wrong. His descriptions depict nurturing parents who took care to see that their sons were educated, well traveled, and aware of historical events when they occurred.

> I was born on May 8, 1856, in the second or third house, I believe, north of Lafayette Avenue on the west side of Carlton Avenue, Brooklyn.
>
> I have only vague memories of that home, for about 1860 or 1861 Father bought the house at 117 Lafayette Avenue [later No. 114], which was the family home until the death of both my parents.

Snow talks of his early school life in Brooklyn at an English and French school on Lafayette Avenue.

He recalled the Civil War and his father's announcement that Lee had surrendered.

Ed and I lay down on the dining room floor and kicked with delight. But a few days afterward came the tragic news of the assassination of President Lincoln.

On the occasion of his funeral procession through New York, I was taken to witness the event from a store window on Broadway.

He recalled hearing Charles Dickens read A Christmas Carol at Plymouth Church in 1868, where he came to know Lyman Abbott and Henry Ward Beecher. He wrote of pleasant memories of childhood times spent with family.

Every summer father took us to the country for the vacation time and one of my most pleasant recollections is that of a summer visit to West Point.

An officer gave father cards for Edward and me to attend the cadet ball.

The honored guest of the affair was President Grant, then at the height of his renown as the commander-in-chief of the Union armies during the war.

I led Edward about the edge of the hall and up to the President's platform. There I explained to him that we had no one to present us and we concluded to present ourselves.

He responded, "Why boys, I am glad you did so and he took Ed on one side and me on the other."

In 1873, Snow's parents took both of the boys out of Brooklyn Polytechnic Institute for an exotic fifteen-month trip around the world, including destinations in Europe, Russia, Turkey, Asia Minor, and the Middle East. In Palestine, he and Edward rode horses while their mother was transported on a palanquin, which was a litter that was carried between two mules.

Snow's description is reminiscent of his account of his exciting adventure rafting on the Magdalena River in Colombia years later.

Did Snow really love Anna as he so sensitively wrote in poems and letters home to the Snow children, or did he love the idea of warm and caring family members who surrounded their prominent father? His disappearance and his abandonment of his family suggest narcissism.

His first two returns to the United States were in 1909 and 1911. He was aware that he had returned when the family was living in Europe.

There is no record that he saw his family again until his visit in 1925. There are ship passenger records of his visits in 1909, 1911, 1925-1926, 1929, and 1931. The final time he saw Anna was in 1931. One of the surviving descendants recalls Snow visiting sometime after Anna's death. Snow was introduced to the grandchildren as Mr. Clark. He wore a beard as a disguise.

While he never put them out of his mind, there is no indication that he was overwrought about being away from the family. Snow's first son David was only three and a half years old when he died. It was tragic but there was no sign that Snow bore it with anything other than resilience, as he did with the early adulthood death of his brother Edward Leslie and the early death of his first daughter Marion.

Constance came to resent his actions when she matured and had been through extensive therapy. In her letters to siblings, she recalled proudly the better times, sharing her recollections of other men showing deference and respect to her father.

When she was invited to a celebration honoring Snow at Polytechnic, Constance reminded the family that Snow had been respected and was always regarded as a gentleman of intellect and great integrity.

Today, Snow remains an honored former valedictorian, president, and chairman at Poly. His service got him acclaim at a second observance on the school's 150th anniversary. His substantial contributions were included in a book about the school's history that Jeffery L. Rodengen wrote.

Snow credited himself with changing the school's charter so that it could accept financial gifts and endowments. It had been unable to do that under its old charter. Rodengen's book, however, states that after five years as chairman, Snow left the school with four hundred thousand dollars in debt.

Constance also wrote diaries. In them, she eventually concluded that Snow had treated the family terribly. She mocked his demands over the years for weekly letters from the children.

Snow's fascination and attraction to famous people suggests his pretentious nature.

Andrew Carnegie's first introduction to Snow occurred when Carnegie was funding a near six-million-dollar library merger in New York City while Snow was serving on the board of one of the libraries.

Reexamining a draft of the merger that Snow had put together, the four Carnegie representatives discovered a third section that they hadn't seen before. They noticed it just as a vote of approval was about to be taken.

The section in question dismissed the representatives from the library board. They charged Snow with bad faith.

Snow's only explanation was that they misunderstood the meaning of the agreement and their dismissal was "permissive, not mandatory."

A lunch at Delmonico's lasted two-and-one-half hours, and Snow was so familiar with every facet of the so-called Morgan Bill that he could recite it. One of the four Carnegie representatives revealed that Snow had never mentioned the section about their dismissals from the board. Further meetings eventually resolved the matter.

Seth Low, the second mayor of New York, eventually forced Snow to resign from the library board over differences.

The chameleon's financial dependence on Allen was a result of a friendship that went back years. In 1897, Snow served as an usher at Allen's wedding.

Grant Hugh Browne of Flint & Company was among his first acquaintances in Venezuela. Browne and his company had been developing business in Venezuela for five years when they met.

Browne would become a well-known figure in New York, London, and Caracas. Beyond his ownership of several companies, he was a boxing promoter, a horseman, and a racing enthusiast. However, his fortune declined again in 1919, when he was convicted with three other men of trying to defraud the US government when they tried to obtain thirty million dollars in military munitions for three hundred thousand dollars.

Browne was called the instigator in the plot and had approached a military officer to help them carry out their plans from the inside. *Orange County* [NY] *Times-Press,* June 10, 1919; *New York Times,* June 8, 1919. Browne's obituary in the

Middletown [NY] *Daily Herald* on March 11, 1925, credited him with having made and lost three fortunes in the Midwest before coming to New York.

When Clark read in *National Geographic* of an appeal by the United States Navy for field glasses for use during the First World War, he wrote to Franklin Delano Roosevelt, who was then the assistant secretary of the Navy, and he sent him a pair of binoculars.

FDR wrote back thanking him. FDR assured him that they would be returned, along with one dollar for the rental fee. When he returned the binoculars, he sent an official statement of thanks and a more personal letter.

Clark's visit to the United States in 1929 began with a voyage to Europe and a stay with Sir Henry and Lady Beaumont, whom he'd met and befriended in Caracas. Setting off for London on September 7, 1929 at the age of seventy-three, he arrived in London on September 26 after stopping at Port of Spain, Trinidad, and Barbados.

At Barbados, he went ashore to search for records of his grandfather's family sailing from England to America. It turned out a hurricane had destroyed the records.

Recalling his trip, Clark wrote:

> From Barbados, a voyage of thirteen days brought us to Plymouth, from which port our first American ancestors sailed in the little Mayflower on the 6th of September 1620, just three hundred and nine years previously.
>
> I spent a day with my English friends, Mr. and Mrs. Risch, at their home in Paignton, not far from Plymouth; and arrived at London on September 26.

Clark's itinerary also called for a stop on the South Coast to visit the Beaumonts, who were residing at their country home Stanswood House at Fawley. His extended time in England lasted until October 9, when he set sail from Southampton for New York. He retained a photograph of himself at the estate.

A 1929 pamphlet on the progress that the Venezuelan government had made under the rule of Gómez paid for the trip. The Spanish translation of the article was carried in serial form in *El Nuevo Diario* in Caracas on successive days in April.

The English translation, Clark recounted, received wide circulation inside and outside of Venezuela. Gómez sent him a note thanking him for the article and expressing "deep gratitude for Mr. Clark's constant proofs of friendship and sympathy toward this republic, its government and General Gómez's person."

The State Department was informed of the trip and the circumstances surrounding it in a dispatch dated December 24, 1929. Engert, serving as the chargé at Caracas, informed the department about it.

Referring to a query from the Office of Secretary of State, Engert replied that in regard to the article on "Venezuela and Her Progressive Ruler, I have the honor to report that I am very reliably informed that Mr. Clark received from General Juan Vicente Gómez the sum of twenty-five thousand [c. five thousand dollars] as a present for writing this article, which has been used for propaganda purposes."

The chameleon's crime and disappearance were as improbable as his entanglements with revolutionists while serving in the US legation. His activities were borne out by records of the US State Department, Army Military Intelligence Division, and the Office of Naval Intelligence. Other accounts described when and where his path intruded into the history of his times.

A more rational man would have opted for a safer and un-eventful life in Venezuela. A more rational man would not have drawn attention to himself.

Snow took five trips back to New York. He took most of these trips without a passport, and he traveled on all trips but the one from England on Red D line steamers docking in Brooklyn. This was foolhardy, particularly in 1909 and 1911.

His longest associations were with Doyle and Gómez. These re-lationships were outgrowths of his needs. Their friendships were beneficial to Clark, including landing him in 1918 the job at the Caribbean Petroleum Company, where he worked for more than a decade. Doyle never knew his real name.

Nothing, however, would compare to Clark's relationship with Gómez. The relationship started with his early efforts for con-cessions. Snow befriended him and eventually brought Addison McKay to him. Their relationship resulted in the formation of their business corporations with the dictator.

Snow was openly accepting of the tyrant's outrages against Venezuelans, including Peñaloza. He dismissed it as though noth-ing else was to be expected.

Archival Research in the United States

Much of the information about Venezuela and its govern-ment comes from the records of the US State Department, the US Army Military Intelligence Division, and the US Office of Naval Intelligence. These groups have many predispositions. Included are descriptions of bubonic plague and the Castro government's mishandling of the disease. They also described Gómez's evils, the conditions of streets in Caracas, the number of cars in Caracas, and the building that housed the consulate at La Guaira.

State Department Record Groups (RG) 59, RG 84, and M366, which are located at Archives II in College Park, Maryland, were a primary source. Much academic research has focused on RG 59 because of its organization. Archivists tend to direct researchers there. I found RG 84 of more use. It was more eclectic but also more time-consuming. Military Intelligence Division records are marked RG 165.

Other frequently used records at Archives II:
Foreign Relations of the United States
Registers of the Department of State 1900-1916, 1933
Records of the War Trade Board, RG 182
FBI Investigative Case Files, RG 65

Other frequently used archival sources in the United States:
Records of the Office of Naval Intelligence, RG 38, Archives I, Washington, DC
Brooklyn Historical Society
Brooklyn Public Library, archives of the *Brooklyn Eagle*, now complete online
Chestnut Hill, PA, Historical Society
Columbus Memorial Library, Organizations of American States, Leo S. Rowe, Manuscript Collection
Coon Public Library, Princeton, Kentucky, McGoodwin
Georgetown University Library, Cornelius Van Engert Papers
Ellis Island Foundation, Ship Passenger Lists
Herkimer County, NY, Historical Society, Rudolf Dolge family and Dolgeville
Library of Congress, Wilbur John Carr Papers
New York Historical Society
New York State Archives

Riverfront Library, Yonkers Public Library
Steamboat Historical Society of America
Steamship Historical Society of America
Venezuelan Embassy, Washington, DC

Archival Research in Caracas:
Boletín del Archivo Histórico de Miraflores
Archivo Histórico del Ministerio de Relaciones Exteriores o Casa Amarilla

Archival Research in UK:
The National Archives, British Foreign Office, Metropolitan Police Archives
General Register Office
British Newspaper Library [*London Times*]

Family Recollections/Materials:
Clark's Four Journals
Papers of Constance Snow Dallas

ACKNOWLEDGMENTS

I am grateful to a number of people for their help. Researcher Christine Thomas of Croydon Surrey, UK, [twiglet.thomas@tiscali.co.uk] unearthed Benjamin Pengelly's later criminal activities after his return to England. Thomas also insightfully added information on British ministers, including their distain for McGoodwin.

Arriving in Caracas from Paris on the same day as me in 2006, Hector Pérez Marchelli met me at the airport. He and his entourage spent several days leading me around the city and nearby towns that figured in the book. My thanks go out to him and his minders, including Straw Hat (TV producer Amador Clark) and Sky King, both of whom served as my security and helped me retrace the escape route that Clark used to spirit General Peñaloza out of the country. The railway down the mountain no longer exists, but remnants of tracks and bridges over plunging ravines remain. I also thank Hector, a Caracas-based writer, researcher, and editor, for information from the diaries of Oraletta Stokes, Ralph Arnold's sister-in-law. These diaries are archived at Huntington Library in San Marino, California. I also thank him for his many readings and corrections in the manuscript.

Andres Duarte Vivas of Caracas was kind enough to invite me to a dinner at his home for an event to celebrate the translation of a book by historian and author Dr. Judith Ewell. Her books include *Venezuela and the United States/From Monroe's Doctrine to Petroleum's Empire.* Like Hector, Andres provided guidance through Venezuela's past, including his recollections of his grandfather's escape from the country by the same rail route as that of General Peñaloza. Antonio Xavier de Breu accumulated material from a variety of Venezuelan archives, and he located the houses where Clark, Carmen, and Chip lived. He also found the cemetery location where Clark and Chip were buried [Cemetery Certificate. *Ocupó la bóveda, No. 1324, del Sur, Cuerpo 2, Sección 5*].

One neighbor recalled Carmen and provided the information that her brothers lived at one of the houses after her death.

In searching through the Archivo Histórico del Ministerio de Relaciones Exteriores o Caso Amarilla and Palacio de Miraflores Archives, Antonio discovered Clark's applications for the Maracaibo Bay dredging concession. He also found two lighthouse projects and details of Venezuela's intent to use McGoodwin as its lobbyist in Washington.

Scholar and author Dr. Brian S. McBeth of St. Antony's College, University of Oxford, offered many useful suggestions that led to book revisions. He also shared pertinent information, especially about the Gómez era and the early development of Venezuela's oil industry, which he has written about extensively.

Dr. William M. Sullivan, who is an author and a scholar, searched his voluminous records several times for answers to my incessant queries. He provided occasional comic relief, for which I remain grateful.

My thanks to Jean McKee of Washington, DC, and Cheshire, Connecticut, who was always generous with her time, her genealogical expertise, and her contacts at the State Department. Jean's great-great uncle, David Brooks, was the father of Anna Snow.

Also, my lasting thanks to Constance Millet of Utica, New York, as well as George Dallas of Concord, Massachusetts. They are siblings. Their mother was Constance, who was the daughter of Henry and Anna. I also thank Les Paternotte. His mother was Anne Snow, who was the daughter of Henry and Anna. Les appeared at my door one day with a story to tell.

Dr. Manuel Caballero is now deceased. He devoted much of a day with Hector and me in the dining room of the Hotel Avila in Caracas.

The day before, I attended the dedication of Dr. Ewell's book translation. Dr. Caballero was among five Venezuelan scholars and authors speaking. Hector informed me that he was regarded as an expert on Gómez and his rule.

Caballero was a distinguished writer, scholar, and television personality who was living in Caracas. He was seventy-eight years old at the time of the interview.

I was barely mobile. I had severe sinus allergies, and I couldn't quit coughing. I was starting to feel that my first venture to Caracas was a failure. However, I approached him after the speeches were over to inquire about Gómez.

It led to an astonishing discovery after I asked him, "Did you ever hear of a guy named Clark?" Dr. Caballero's eyes widened. "Mr. Clark? Yes. He married my aunt, Carmen."

It was at that time that I noticed the same last name, a not uncommon one in Venezuela.

Surprised, I prodded him. "They had a son?"

Dr. Caballero then answered, "Chip. I got his clothes when he died."

I was stunned.

Researchers at both National Archives locations were extremely helpful and giving of their time. I apologize for too many requests to go up (or was it down) into the stacks and my highly favored record group, RG 84.

Plymouth Church and its historians and researchers helped me time and again. And the staff of the Brooklyn Public Library provided much needed materials and guidance to both its printed and online archives, which include the library of the *Brooklyn Eagle*.

Finally, my thanks go to the staff at the Hotel Avila in Caracas for their patience and goodwill as I instructed them about how to mix a martini. I thank them for learning so well.

To Venezuelans of every stripe, I hope and pray you can find your way out of the morass.

ABOUT THE AUTHOR

T he author is an award-winning journalist who held senior positions at the Miami Herald, the Washington Star, and Newsday. During his twenty years at Newsday the newspaper won eleven Pulitzer Prizes, including the spot news award for the crash of TWA Flight 800 off the Long Island coast. When he left Newsday in 2001 he was vice president and managing editor/Operations.

He is a past chairman of the Board of Directors of the Guide Dog Foundation for the Blind, Inc. in Smithtown, Long Island, New York. He is an entertaining public speaker who has represented Newsday and the Guide Dog Foundation in speaking engagements many times.

He lives with his wife and two golden retrievers, Savannah and Boomer T. Bailey, on the Eastern Shore of Maryland.

He can be contacted at bbrandt1@atlanticbb.net and www.booksbybrandt.com. Also look for us on Facebook, Youtube and Twitter.